Green Logic

Ecopreneurship, Theory and Ethics

Robert Isaak

For
Sonya, Andrew
and the grandchildren of the world

green
logic

Robert Isaak

Ecopreneurship,
Theory
and
Ethics

KUMARIAN
PRESS

Green Logic: Ecopreneurship, Theory and Ethics

Published 1999 in the United States of America by Kumarian Press, Inc.,
14 Oakwood Avenue, West Hartford, Connecticut 06119-2127 USA.

Published 1998 in the United Kingdom by **Greenleaf** Publishing, Broom
Hall, 8-10 Broomhall Road, Sheffield S10 2DR, UK.

Printed in the United Kingdom

Library of Congress Cataloging-in-Publication data

Isaak, Robert A.
    Green logic: ecopreneurship, theory, and ethics / Robert
    Isaak.
    p. cm.
    Includes bibliographical references and index.
    ISBN 1-56549-095-9 (pbk. : alk. paper)
    1. Environmental sciences—Philosophy. 2. Environmental ethics.
3. Entrepreneurship—Philosophy. 4. Environmental justice. I.
Title
    GE40 .I73 1999
    179'.1—ddc21

                                                        98-43218
                                                            CIP

ISBN 1-56549-095-9

03 02 01 00 99   5   4   3   2   1
First Printing 1999

Contents

Preface

Economic activity imposes increasing costs on the global environment. The lack of progress being made in environmental management is often not as much a question of economics, technology or even of interest as it is of perception, assumptions and how one approaches problems. Sometimes we need to shake up our way of thinking, just as the child does the kaleidoscope, mixing the colors in order see the world differently (that is, in greener shades). This short book seeks to highlight a few key questions regarding entrepreneurship and sustainability in terms of motivation, government intervention and ethics. It is best viewed as a series of interrelated thought experiments or hypothetical solutions. The aim is to uncover what 'green logic' means and what it takes to motivate entrepreneurs to design and start up green businesses. Or, alternatively, how can one steer a business away from activities harmful to the environment, which may in the long term make it less competitive and, in any case, lower its respectability in the eyes of one's grandchildren. Albert Schweizer once said that setting an example is not just a factor that leads to influence: it is the only factor.

The complexity of environmental issues can be a deterrent to understanding them. To cut through complexity, it sometimes helps to be playful. I discovered that playing with ideas from the fields of creativity, entrepreneurship, management and political philosophy makes environmental concerns come alive; their relevance to the cutting edge of competitiveness and globalization becomes more transparent.

I would like to acknowledge briefly just a few of the people who helped me on the way to completing this adventure in green ideas: Günter Liesegang, Malte Faber, Reiner Manstetten, Till Requate, Jürgen Siebke, Dieter Fahrion, Frank Jöst, Armin Schmutzler and Helmut Less provided inspiration, ideas and help at thc Alfred Weber Institute of the University of Heidelberg where they kindly took me in for a year as a Fulbright scholar. I learned much from my students there in our seminar on Ecological Theory, Competitiveness and Environmental Entrepreneurship, as illustrated here by the EMAS chapter, co-authored with Alexander Keck, now at Cambridge. Vicci Hottenrott helped me wind up the translation of this chapter and other numerous details with good-natured energy and competence. I am also grateful to Jackie Womack and her staff for helping sort out the formatting. Dieter Schultz reinforced my interest in Thoreau and Dieter Roth helped with questionnaire methodology. Peter Eichhorn of the University of Mannheim inspired me with his example. Dieter Wagner at the University of Potsdam orchestrated a surge of stimulation in his conference on transitional economies. Manfred Kirchgeorg provided other insights at our colloquium at the Leipzig Graduate School of Management. Reiner Rohr and Barbara Ischinger effectively steered the financial and intellectual support of the Fulbright Commission. Colleagues at Pace University in New York, Larry Bridwell, Greg Julian, David Rahni, Peter Hoefer and Arthur Centonze, always provided an ear, if not quiet inspiration for sustaining my interest in sustainability. My wife Gudrun, daughter Sonya and son Andrew helped to ensure that this book would not become longer. And John Stuart at Greenleaf Publishing provided the faith, patience and support that brought the manuscript to fruition.

R.A.I.

Introduction
Globalization and Ecopreneurship

A human being can stand only in one place at a time. This point of departure appears to be arbitrary. But the stand the individual takes should ideally be based on an Archimedean point, a position that permits maximum leverage not only for the life-chances of the individual but for the life-chances of his or her children and children's children. The purpose of this book is to demonstrate that the ideal point of leverage is grounded upon green logic.

Green logic is the logic of long-term, risk-reducing environmentalism. It assumes that the earth and its resources are finite, while human desires and demands are infinite. Green logic thus involves postponing some short-term gratification for the sake of long-term satisfaction in contemplating the needs of one's children and grandchildren. Economically, it can best be understood as a philosophy of saving, innovation and investment.

Globalization is concerned with massive, competitive pressure for short-term adaptation: the managers of instant financial and information flows rally the masses to change instantly in order to keep up with the latest twists in technology, to maximize short-term returns, to stimulate macro-economic growth and to hedge against insecurity. Green logic is often represented as a counterpoint of humanism, cultural integrity and civilized planning. However, qualitative competitiveness must be 'sustainable' in all senses of that word. A notion of life-chances that goes beyond mere material needs does not contradict green logic, but incorporates it. 'The good life' has a green beginning. And green entrepreneurship, or ecopreneurship, is the means to sustainable competitiveness.

Coping with Globalization

The process of globalization implies that the twenty-first century is already upon us. Future global trends are manifest in the present. Adaptation should have begun yesterday. Globalization evokes fear in the masses of people and courage in a minority of entrepreneurial innovators. To become established, green logic will ultimately depend on transforming the courage of the entrepreneur from a natural short-term concern with survival into a richer, long-term vision that helps to create a humanistic and civilized development which respects the limits of the earth's resources.

The human problem lies not so much in knowing what the trends are that constitute globalization, but in individual and collective adaptation to them on a daily basis. We are framed by our old habits. The more we experience global change, the greater the temptation to go back to these habits of the past for comfort, much as the child goes back home to the parents after some traumatic personal experience. These habits I refer to as 'maintenance' patterns, or efforts to maintain and stabilize systems of the past. Such habits, which preoccupy most managers, stem from understandable concerns with maximizing the efficiency, stability and reduction of risk within the organization or 'the maintenance base' (or 'home base'). Restructuring for the sake of consolidation is an example.

Maintenance patterns are characterized by limiting perceptions and collective learning to traditional schemata—habitual prototypes of meaning that steer behavior. Such schemata include 'order' and 'risk reduction' in Germany, 'individual freedom' in the United States and the United Kingdom, and 'shame' in Japan. These schemata serve as branding irons on our perceptions, limiting our imaginations to routine cultural habits (see Fig. 1). In contrast, what we require for effective collective adaptation are 'creative' and 'entrepreneurial' patterns that use existing schemata or perceptual lenses as paths to create new products, markets, jobs, socioeconomic and political solutions—as illustrated in Chapter 1.

Thus, traditional cultural schemata are overwhelmed by the pressures of globalization. Conservative psychological reactions or 'maintenance' modes are understandable from a viewpoint of human coping. But these collective responses need to be redirected for the sake of entrepreneurial innovation, job creation and environmental sustainability. And, to do this, one must break things down into smaller pieces: (i) global trends; (ii) obstacles that block adaptation to these trends; (iii) changes to help people adapt in a sustainable way; and (iv) a universal ethical stance that makes green entrepreneurship comprehensible as a common-sense risk-reducing strategy of long-term savings and investment consistent with sustainability.

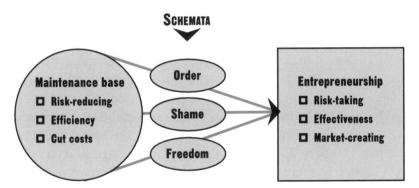

Figure 1: **Maintenance Base**

A. Global Trends

Financial, technological and transportation revolutions have spawned a global 'placeless society', which investment banker William Knoke, President of the Harvard Capital Group, has defined as 'the Age of Everything-Everywhere' (Knoke 1996) where people and goods often move instantaneously from one location to another. Social structures formerly based on the primacy of place are undermined by globalization. Free-rider behavior, or the temptation to maximize individual or collective interests by pushing the costs onto someone else, becomes the norm, rather than the exception (see Chapter 1, §A1).

As illustrated by the Internet, the world has become an open cafeteria of options and information. 'Locationless commerce' characterizes proliferating electronic and virtual markets; resulting virtual communities change how companies develop, price and promote their products. Money flows in and out of countries and funds instantaneously without controls. Central bankers, governments, large institutions and companies are playing a permanent game of catch-up, pretending to be in control by catching the right wave of the markets at the right time. Governments and banks approve and subsidize large company mergers which arm themselves for global competition by eliminating workers, which raises the price of their stocks and their ability to attract capital. But the legitimacy of the elites leading these established organizations is low, since the masses, sooner or later, see through the puppet show. Habermas's crisis of legitimacy, which was once left-wing heresy, has now become commonplace wisdom (Habermas 1971). Market research agencies in the United States have charted a trend of annual declines in the loss of trust in business leaders, illustrating that the loss of legitimacy is not just limited to managers in the public sector. Harvard political scientist Samuel Huntington's work (Huntington 1993) confirms the loss of legitimacy in established institutions at all levels in the late twentieth century. However, Habermas's recent proposals for a *Weltinnenpolitik* (a domestic world politics) investing in the United Nations in order to recover the legitimacy lost and aiming for *Die Einbeziehung des Anderen* ('the bringing-in of "the others" ') constitute a noble edifice of social justice without economic feet.

There is another trend, not unrelated to social justice: the revolt of the masses against global change in order to preserve the past in the present. Unions strike to protect existing jobs and benefits threatened by corporate and governmental restructuring; students protest to keep university fees from going up; civil servants demonstrate to counter proposals to cut back their pensions; farmers and poets lament the loss of the sense of place and commitment to local roots (see Chapter 2). All of these groups represent a 'New Psychological Conservatism', an example of which is 'the 401K generation': the significant group of baby-boomers in the United States more concerned with maximizing their private pensions than anything else. The same is true of Japanese economic policy in the 1990s, which, until 1998, was more concerned with funding the retirement of the fast-aging population than with stimulating consumption at home in order to help pull other Asian neighbors out of the malaise stemming from currency crisis by buying their products.

Resistance to change for the sake of principles is, of course, the very definition of character, integrity or ἀρετή (honor). But, often, if I go down in flames for the sake of principle, my spouse and children suffer. Postmodern character can no longer be a short-term burning of bridges and standing-up only for one's own rights at all costs. The concept of character must be extended to cover the rights of one's children and children's children—stretched, in short, to meet the requirements of sustainable development. Here's the philosophical rub: to the extent that my character is defined in terms merely of defending my job, my past, my tuition and my old way of life, regardless of the costs imposed on my children and grandchildren, my notion of character has become illegitimate and is no longer viable.

So what global trends must I then take into account in order to create a viable future for my children and their children?

- ☐ **First**, global trends towards privatization and corporate restructuring will make almost all full-time jobs temporary. Therefore, existentially, one has little to lose (and a sense of integrity to gain) by developing any job's potential for environmental responsibility or targeting. Financial security, however, can no longer merely be job-based. Looking for wealth in one's take-home pay from a job is like looking for gold in a salt mine. I will maintain or increase my prosperity only by investments outside my workplace. As government and corporate benefits are cut back, I need to invest in things from local business start-ups to socially responsible international companies that pass a 'green screen' in order to provide financial security for myself, my children and their children. Countries with low rates of adult ownership in the stock market, such as the 6% rate in Germany, 16% in France and even the 25% in the United Kingdom (compared with 43% in the United States) will have to change their behavior radically in order to cover future family financial needs (although this pattern seems to be shifting). Or, if, alternatively, governments want to steer towards a stock-based, universal credit economy that creates green jobs rather than continuing to stimulate the paper entrepreneurship of merely making money from money, national tax incentives will have to be shifted accordingly.

- ☐ **Second**, I need to be computer-literate but with a light touch. I need to be able communicate and operate globally and locally without becoming so absorbed in information technology and data-processing that I forget to live and interact with others and the natural world. As Swiss novelist Max Frisch put it, 'Technology is the art of so arranging life that you do not have to experience it.'[1] Human depth requires dwelling in a real world rather than in a vicarious existence.

---

1. Personal conversation.

▣ **Third**, I need to realize that, while globalization drives one to placelessness, human health and integrity demand arbitrary roots or a home base in one specific place, or perhaps ideally two for variety. While some travel may be arbitrarily open, other travel must be arbitrarily fixed and routine in order to give a structure to life and a deeper meaning and commitment to specific people and communities.

▣ **Fourth**, I need to recognize that, for most people in the world, unemployment and underemployment will be the major issues of the future, but, for the sake of my children and grandchildren, I must help to solve the problem of unemployment for myself and for others in a manner that is environmentally responsible and sustainable. The scarcity of quality jobs (or what economists call 'positional goods') will drive up their value and social status whether or not one needs them personally; I must redefine my job in green terms and share it with others who are without work (see Chapter 1, §C). I can adapt my work to maximize its green content—tilting it towards recycling, natural ingredients, waste and energy reduction, environmentally friendly suppliers and green job-creating investments. And I can look locally for people who need work or direction with whom to share these explicitly green activities. Often, by coordinating such efforts with non-profit and public service organizations, I may cut my costs and enjoy a multiplier effect in terms of my marketing objectives.

▣ **Fifth**, I need to know the limits of my own culture well enough to transcend them in order to pull in and adapt to the positive contributions of other cultures. As an American, I can learn the value of social capital formation from the Germans and self-effacement for the sake of a goal or state of consciousness from the Japanese. As a German, I can learn the value of cultivating flexibility and individual freedom in organizations for the sake of creativity and innovation from the Americans, and I can learn the value of spontaneous living and existential humor from the

French, the Greeks and the Italians. As a Brit, I can learn that the nature of solidarity in Germany and Asia is different than that of the organic individualism I have experienced and is characterized by long-term group commitments that are unlikely to change quickly, no matter what markets may demand. North Americans, Europeans, Asians and Africans can learn from belated Costa Rican efforts to put biodiversity first as a social value. And people from these same cultures can all learn to get inside the culture of Islam to discover the value it has to offer in order to head off cultural apartheid, not to mention terrorism. Each human being, in short, must become a renaissance person, a personal repertoire of multicultural agency, embracing risks and other cultures for the sake of global sustainable development.

B. Obstacles to Coping with Global Trends

The Case of Europe in General and Germany in Particular

To the extent the Maastricht Treaty of 1991 (committing European Union member nations to a unified European currency, central bank, social and defense policy) serves to stabilize the old rather than to create the new, it may become an obstacle to coping with global change. At a time when the clearest economic priority is job creation, the focus on tight money for the sake of meeting the criteria for the 'Euro' (the unified European currency scheduled to appear by 2002) appears to be counterproductive in the short term. While the Asian financial crisis of the late 1990s and the peaking of the American boom cycle may lead investors to shift capital to a stable Euro for the sake of diversification, this capital will not automatically be steered to job creation, much less to green job creation. And, with the

Euro's introduction, the European Central Bank initially will have to lean towards tight, hard money in order to reassure skeptical financial markets which are bound to test the new currency—thus restraining economic growth and job creation.

People cannot focus on too many priorities at once: strong elements in our perceptions drive out weaker, more dependent elements, creating stable loops (see Chapter 1, §B). One such loop, for example, is the time-destroying perceptual chain linking hard work to higher income to more consumption to hard work. The tilt of the Maastricht Treaty, its 1997 Amsterdam successor and the stable Euro agenda towards non-job-producing economic policy in the short run serves to distract government policy-makers from focusing sufficiently on policies that do produce new jobs in general and green jobs in particular.

The entire process of European integration can be questioned. Internally, it may distract national governments in Europe from decentralizing strategies that may be more efficient, flexible and conducive to job creation. The Eurocrats are necessarily focused more on harmonizing what is rather than on creating what is not—what is called 'going deeper before going broader'. Insecure about their 'maintenance base', the members of the European Union are trying to get their own house in order before they begin to adapt to the radical changes that are likely to be then long overdue if they want to cope competitively in the world economy. Externally, the European integration process may inadvertently distract the Europeans into becoming Eurocentric when the critical need may be to shift to understanding non-European cultures—towards learning Chinese, for example.

Furthermore, academically, studies of integration rarely bear much fruit: they seem to be theoretically diffuse in the middle range and often suffer from either undue Europhoria or Euro-pessimism—both forms of regional provincialism. Rather than becoming more competitive by joining the European Union, nations may find that Euroregulations actually get in the way of competitive adaptation. Of course, in the early twenty-first century European political leaders may surprise us and come up with institutional innovations that truly make for a dynamic and effective United States of Europe. But whether or not the existing cast of political characters has the imaginative intellectual capacity and political will to bring this about is an open question.

Rather than more regulation, in the financial sector the Europeans, and particularly the Germans, need more flexibility. Empirical economic research by Daniel Hamermesh demonstrates that about one out of three new jobs created comes from a new start-up firm (Hamermesh 1993). Yet the regulatory barriers and difficulty in obtaining venture capital frustrate many from attempting to start their own businesses. To prevent a potential bankruptcy from wiping out a person's total private financial existence requires founding a limited or GmbH (*Gesellschaft mit beschränkter Haftung*) firm. But the thresholds to qualify for a GmbH are high, including an investment by the founder of DM50,000 (half of which can be made up of non-cash security). And, should an entrepreneur fail in founding a firm the first time around, there are bureaucratic obstacles to trying again and credit becomes almost impossible to obtain. Existing policy, in short, fosters risk reduction, not risk-taking.

If we look empirically at what has happened since reunification in the Rhine–Neckar *Dreieck* (triangle) we discover that, immediately after 1989, the number of new start-ups increased (see Fig. 2). But then the numbers fell to fewer than half the number of start-ups between 1990 and 1992, increasing significantly again in 1993 and then falling again thereafter and leveling off at about 70% of the 1990 high. In the new German states or *Länder*, the number of start-ups peaked in July 1990 and the rate of increase then flattened out through 1994. The numbers are better in the new German states but, given the importance of fostering start-ups to bring down the escalating unemployment rate, it is curious that there is no systematic federal data collected on start-ups in the *Bundesrepublik*. Moreover, there is no central collection of comparative statistics on European start-ups in the EU in Brussels. Those who collect data on start-ups are forced to go to work for credit-rating agencies, such as CREDITREFORM in Germany. The message is clear: even

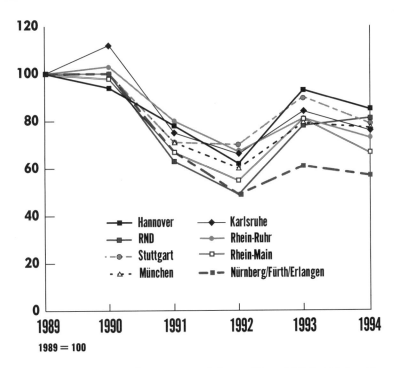

Figure 2: **The Development of Start-Ups 1989–94 in the Rhein–Neckar Region of Germany**
Source: Egeln *et al.* 1996

if politicians now and then praise start-ups, they do not follow through in practice. And since many of the start-ups deliberately stay below ten workers to avoid being obligated to set up a *Betriebsrat* (firm council), which can heavily influence hiring and firing, unions generally ignore start-ups as a solution to the unemployment they are always lamenting. And German universities, for their part, do little about teaching entrepreneurship or legitimizing start-ups as a career goal, thereby becoming part of the problem rather than of the solution.[2]

2. One of several exceptions that prove the rule was the successful seminar on founding businesses offered for the first time at the University of Heidelberg in 1997 in cooperation with the Industrie- und Handelskammer Rhein-Neckar. (The alliance concept *outside* the university here is no accident!)

Empirical studies have clearly identified a significant role of start-ups in fostering technological innovation (see Chapter 1, §A). Nevertheless, German university structures and curricula do not encourage creativity or risk-taking. Contrast this with American university programs at MIT and Stanford, which not only provide venture capital for student start-ups, but teach entrepreneurial skills and provide access to advice from retired entrepreneurs to help prevent bankruptcies from the outset.

Both university and government bureaucracies make the possibility of supporting green start-ups unnecessarily difficult: environmental economics programs are housed separately from small business programs in universities, and in the *Industrie- und Handelskammer* the department that provides advice on environmental programs is separate from that which discusses support for start-ups.

But what about assuring the environmental responsibility of businesses just starting up?

The EMAS program for European environmental management certification by the European Union, the way it is presently designed, is more relevant to medium-sized and large firms that have the management capacity, capital and time than it is to small, job-creating start-ups. (The same applies to the ISO 14001 international guidelines.) The thrust is towards eco-efficiency in existing systems rather than in system transformation in order to create new green–green businesses (those that start up green from scratch)—as is demonstrated in Chapter 3 in interviews with German firms that have received EMAS certification.

C. Proposed Solutions for Europe

The solutions to adapting to global change in Germany and Europe imply a cultural revolution, a movement from maintaining the past to creating a decentralized, entrepreneurial, flexible future with a commitment to lifelong learning and spiritual renewal (see Chapter 5). Financially, European banks and capital markets will not be able to maintain their global competitiveness without redesigning for flexibility, transparency and easy access to stock market transactions by the general public. The Euro alone is no panacea for the absence of competitiveness.

Technologically, many universities will have to retool student dormitories and classrooms with computer facilities just in order to cope with the present rather than looking constantly back to the past for guidance. To pay for this restructuring, universities will have to form alliances with private firms and institutes. Learning-by-doing should be booted up to the university level from the *Fachhochschule* (technical schools) if German universities are to increase the odds of earning Nobel prizes in economics on the one hand, and provide useful analysis and training for the unemployment dilemma on the other. For theory and practice have become hopelessly intertwined through the shrinkage of time due to globalization.

Bill Gates, the CEO of Microsoft, has set up a 'hands-on' software research center at Cambridge University in England; such a development is culturally inconceivable in many of the public universities in Germany. Creativity, entrepreneurship and socially responsible risk-taking must be fostered intellectually as well as professionally with a constant stream of visitors (or their video lectures) from all over the world: people who symbolize these values and serve as role models. Learning, after all, has less to do with eliminating failure rates than with speeding up rates of failure. Vicarious experience and learning-by-doing courses aid in this process. The theoretical prowess developed in German universities is all too often not easy to translate into practice, or else the lead-times are just too long for competitiveness in the world economy.

Similarly, in politics, green parties will consistently have to identify with green economic growth rather than leaving job creation and economic growth as issues for other parties. 'Green' must come to mean new buds, surprising, innovative fecundity, and not naïve identification with preserving the old—a strategy that is too defensive. The most successful green–green businesses are system-transforming, socially committed ventures that absorb total time commitment from the founders. They are joyful learning adventures as much as they are businesses (see Chapter 1, §C). They resurrect the Nietzschean hope of creating one's own value, dignity and possibility of finding fulfillment through social action in a spiritually driven process of targeted risk-taking. As Anita Roddick, founder of The Body Shop put it,

> I think the leadership of a company should encourage the next generation not just to follow, but to overtake. The duty of leadership is to put forward ideas, symbols and metaphors of the way it should be done, so that the next generation can work out new and better ways of doing the job (Roddick 1991: 227).

In short, today's politicians would be best advised to foster risk-taking for the sake of job growth through small companies and to risk their own political failure for the sake of replacing themselves with those even more committed to sustainable development.

Examples illustrating green–green businesses or *ecopreneurship* include: The Body Shop, which provides alternatives to cutting down rainforests through buying oils from seeds from indigenous people in Brazil; Ben and Jerry's in the United States, which creates ice cream from all natural ingredients; and Scott Bader, which is a commonwealth as well as a business in the UK, and is described at the end of E.F. Schumacher's book, *Small Is Beautiful* (Schumacher 1973; cf. Chapter 1, §C2). German examples of green–green firms include Spinnrad (a domestic German 'hobby-tech, do-it-yourself textile' firm) and Waschbär (a domestic German company with 4,000 environmentally safe everyday products). To lure people into high-risk, high-commitment green–green undertakings, European governments and the European Commission should target most of their subsidies, tax breaks and transparent promotion for *green–green* start-ups run by *ecopreneurs*—that is, not only businesses that aim at an environmental niche, but those that envision their business designs to be system-transforming, socially committed and technologically up-to-date breakthrough ventures.

D. From Clash of Cultures towards Universal Sustainability

But green–green thinking and ecopreneurship on a widespread level will require transforming existing cultural patterns—radically, in the long term. And cultural schemata—prototypes of meaning—are useful concepts for understanding the clash of cultures or civilizations which Harvard University's Samuel Huntington assures us will dominate the twenty-first century (Huntington 1996). The neo-Confucian modernism of China and the Asian tigers and the widespread growth of the Islamic movement are examples of cultural competition with which Western liberal democratic societies are confronted.

The clashes of culture are of particular significance if we accept the famous Hegelian interpreter Alexander Kojéve's assumption that what is distinctly human is the spiritual in contrast with nature, and the historical in contrast with God (Kojéve 1968). Humans are beings with time in them. Their 'freedom' constitutes recognition of their own contingency and death; their discontent is as temporary as the accident of human consciousness. Excesses of human discontent, pride and disorder are not good for nature and the environment. Kojéve predicts, in short, that, without God, secular liberal humanism is not viable, that history is an error, and that human beings will end up as equal automatons in fully secularized democratic systems without happiness or dignity but with mere contentment as a goal, not distinguishable from other animals. The emergence of such Western decadence is exactly what makes the God-embracing, anti-secular Islamic movement so powerful, particularly among the poor left out of the promised prosperity of democratic capitalism.

If one does not accept Kojéve's projection, the only alternative appears to be Nietzschean efforts by human beings to counter a godless, secularized universe by creating their own values, their own histories, yes, their own small spiritually and socially driven organizations and companies in order to recover their individual dignity and happiness. Somehow, the functions of entrepreneurship for the sake of economic growth and job creation and trusteeship for the sake of maintaining the integrity of the natural environment must be synthesized in a spiritually driven and socially responsible humanism. We must move *from* a preoccupation with instant present gratification and high risk-taking for the short-term regardless of future consequences (a symptom of decadence in Western democratic liberal societies based on 'creative destruction'), *first to* moderating risk through the greening of existing firms, *then to* focusing risk by creating a society epitomizing green values, and *finally to* radically reducing risk to the natural environment by supporting only green–green ecopreneurship and sustainable economic growth (see Fig. 3). This progression constitutes a collective learning process driven not just by the ecopreneur as a change agent, but by a key paradox: short-term high risk must be taken and

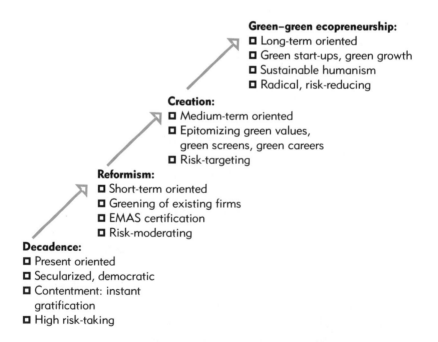

Green–green ecopreneurship:
- ◻ Long-term oriented
- ◻ Green start-ups, green growth
- ◻ Sustainable humanism
- ◻ Radical, risk-reducing

Creation:
- ◻ Medium-term oriented
- ◻ Epitomizing green values, green screens, green careers
- ◻ Risk-targeting

Reformism:
- ◻ Short-term oriented
- ◻ Greening of existing firms
- ◻ EMAS certification
- ◻ Risk-moderating

Decadence:
- ◻ Present oriented
- ◻ Secularized, democratic
- ◻ Contentment: instant gratification
- ◻ High risk-taking

Figure 3: **Green–Green Time and Risk Reduction (or Sustainable Development)**

targeted to found green businesses for the sake of radical long-term environmental risk-reduction (see Chapters 2 and 5).

Last but not least, ethically, we must realize that people of whatever culture cannot be expected to sacrifice their short-term interests for an infinite number of future generations. This is not realistic. Rather let the goal be to think of one's children's children and to ask each evening before going to bed: what have I done today for my grandchildren who may or may not have been born and for the earth they will inherit? As suggested in Chapter 4, this may be the closest we can come to a universal ethical principle for sustainable development—not asking abstractly for the future of the whole human race but merely working daily for a healthy, natural environment for those human beings who are at hand.

Chapter 1
Entrepreneurship, Creativity and Ecodesign

Patterns of creativity and entrepreneurship resulting in environmentally responsible businesses or green economic growth do not emerge by accident. Creativity and entrepreneurship are outgrowths of distinctive processes of collective learning. *Collective learning* is social learning in a specific organizational context, guided by a particular cultural gestalt. This cultural gestalt or tradition selects 'legitimate' patterns of adaptive behavior in managing environmental change that do not undermine cultural integrity. Such cultural patterns are made up of indigenous *schemata*. Schemata are prototypes of meaning used for processing information in a given culture and branding it with particular interpretations. The culture of the United States, for example, is steered by the schema of 'individual freedom' in contrast to the schema of Germany, which brands perceptions in the first instance with the schema of 'order', or in contrast with Japan, which see things traditionally through the schema of 'shame'.

Behind these schemata that shape a society are relevant fictions or utopias which guide its educational system, structure its class system and condition the life-chances, as sociologist Karl Mannheim (1936) demonstrated. These relevant fictions or utopias also set its ideal environmental guidelines for the creation of environmental businesses. That the culture of the United

States is conducive to small entrepreneurial start-ups flows from its preoccupation with individual freedom, just as the German concept of the closed-loop economy for the recycling of parts and packaging is a natural outgrowth of the German schema of order. Or, put another way, in order to break free from their conventional assumption of order to stimulate entrepreneurial start-ups and job creation, the Germans may have to risk more freedom, while, in order to adapt to a viable long-term standard of 'sustainable development', the Americans may have to give up some of their freedom for the sake of social order and more systematic recycling regulations. Other countries such as Singapore or Japan have created economic miracles of growth by targeting their schemata of collective learning on applied economic tasks at decisive moments of global economic growth, financing their would-be 'earthly utopias' through exports or free-riding on conditions outside their limited, partially closed domestic economies. Edward De Bono's conception of 'water logic' (De Bono 1994) or the logic of perception is one way of tapping into the perceptual loops or vital elements of concentration or psychological outgrowths of schemata that work to shape our collective views of creativity, entrepreneurship and sustainable development (Isaak 1997c). But it may be easier to begin on more familiar ground with the logic of the entrepreneur: that little engine of economic growth and job creation.

A. The Logic of the Entrepreneur

Economist Joseph Schumpeter identified the entrepreneur as the vanguard of the process of economic growth, or of what he called the 'creative destruction' that characterizes capitalism (Schumpeter 1950). The word 'entrepreneurship' derives from a French root meaning 'to undertake'. Howard Stevenson at Harvard identifies entrepreneurship as a behavior or process by which individuals pursue opportunities without regard to the resources they currently control. The entrepreneur or 'promoter' is driven by the perception of opportunity or is value-driven, often team-oriented, and relies on performance-based, flat, informal modes of organization. Thus, the logic of the entrepreneur contrasts sharply with that of what Stevenson calls the 'trustee' (and I call 'the maintenance man') who is driven by resources currently controlled, tends towards formalized, promotion-oriented hierarchy in organization, and is security-driven (Stevenson *et al.* 1989; Isaak 1995: 33-34).

American entrepreneur William Lynch interviewed a number of other American entrepreneurs and found that entrepreneurs are: (1) *visionary*, knowing exactly what they want and seeing their object with vivid clarity; (2) *risk-taking* in a way others do not understand, since they see the risk differently; (3) *impatient* in terms of timing, since they already feel it is late; (4) *exhibit salesmanship*, often reversing the conventional order of 'ready, aim, fire' to 'ready, fire, aim'; (5) *are willing to sacrifice* for the cost of entry, having 'fire in the belly'; (6) *view opportunity as love at first sight*, seeing what they want and going for it; (7) *exhibit leadership*; (8) view *credibility as the key to financial leverage*, not credit; (9) *do not see obstacles*, since they are blinded by the objective; (10) *exhibit energy*, an unstoppable need to achieve; and (11) *strive for ownership and control*, their *raison d'être* in terms of motivation (Lynch 1994).

1. The Entrepreneur as Creative Free-Rider

The entrepreneur can be considered to be a creative version of the free-rider (or, in German, *Trittbrettfahrer*—one who used to jump aboard for free on the *Trittbrett* ['stepping board'] or outer wooden step of the old trams or metros that ran above ground in Europe). For, although we may all be free-riders to some extent, as Heidelberg Professor Malte Faber suggested,[3] some free-riders are more motivated than others to take creative risks in order to bring visions into reality. The entrepreneur is, in the words of Robert Schwartz, 'a dreamer who does'

---

3. Personal conversation.

(Kao 1989: 96). Entrepreneurs who start their own businesses may be indifferent as to whether their venture capital comes from Aunt Matilda, the local bank or the state, but, to survive more than a few years, they must systematically reduce their costs by free-riding on public infrastructures, information sources and support wherever they can find it. And the wisest entrepreneurs do not view themselves as risk-takers as much as they do as individuals who specialize in risking *other people's* resources. Stevenson characterized the relationship between risk and reward in the eyes of the entrepreneur as 'You take the risk. I'll take the reward' (Kao 1989: 168).

From the entrepreneur's perspective, of course, the free-rider motive is often not paramount and is offset by other perceptions. He or she may argue: 'I contribute my energies and risk my own investment to bring people a new product, technology or service that they want or need, making the relationship an exchange rather than a free ride.' Or, the entrepreneur may argue, 'The public infrastructures are owned by all and open to all and, since I pay my taxes just like anyone else, I may as well get something back in return for my contribution.' Nevertheless, without the potential for cutting costs in order to make high returns possible, at least in the imagination, the entrepreneur will be unlikely to take the risk of founding a firm in the first place. And, from the collective perspective of society, the free-rider motive is very real from the view of those who do not take the risks nor 'overuse' public infrastructures, even if it is complacency, laziness or the lack of conviction that holds back the majority of people from taking such risks.

2. The Logic of Collective Action

The logic of the entrepreneur cannot become a collective logic without outside intervention. This is because of the way collective logic works.

As Mancur Olson demonstrated in *The Logic of Collective Action* (Olson 1965), free-rider behavior is not only rational but is reinforced in liberal, free-market societies:

Unless the number of individuals is quite small, or unless there is coercion or some other special device to make individuals act in their common interest, *rational, self-interested individuals will not act to achieve their common or group interests* [emphasis original].

For example, if a worker with a family of five hungry children crosses a picket line to work in a factory in order to feed them, he his maximizing his own small-group interest at the expense of the interest of the larger union organization. But, if, the night after he crossed the line to go to work, a brick comes flying through his living room window, an instrument of outside coercion serves to enforce the larger organizational interest and the father will most likely not cross the picket line in the morning for the sake of the security of his family. But, should there be no outside intervention to reinforce the norms and interests of the larger organization, the individual is rationally motivated to maximize his or her own self-interest or family interest, 'free-riding' on the stability provided by the larger organization.

Mancur Olson shows that, 'where small groups with common interests are concerned, *there is a systematic tendency for "exploitation" of the great by the small'* (Olson 1965: 2, 29 [emphasis original]). In a liberal democratic economy, small groups within a larger organization are not rational if they do not maximize their own group interest, even at the expense of the interest of the larger organization if no outside sanctions or interventions to support the values of the larger organization enter the situation. This natural temptation to maximize individual and small-group interest at the expense of larger-group or institutional interest explains why so-called 'intrapreneurship' or entrepreneurship within large companies usually does not work: workers not surprisingly are more concerned with job security than with entrepreneurial risk-taking (Lynch 1994). Of course, the rationality of free-rider motivation also applies within large and established companies that use their economic and political power to reduce their socio-environmental costs at the expense of other small companies and groups. The point here is that only the systematic outside enforcement of norms in terms of incentives or sanctions can be counted on to steer free-rider behavior away from behavior that is harmful to the environment.

If corporate and government organizations fail to intervene to enforce rules of environmental responsibility, rational individuals will be tempted to maximize their own short-term economic and professional interests over green logic or sustainable development within the organizations, 'free-riding' on the delicate ecosystems of the world in which they operate. Of course, the logic of collective action is colored by the culture in which it operates, steered by traditional schemata that legitimize the way entrepreneurial risk-taking is generally viewed. While there are numerous examples of individuals and groups doing things for wider groups at nobody's expense but their own, this altruistic motivation alone is not likely to be widespread enough in modern societies to carry out a systematic program of sustainability.

3. Entrepreneurship across Cultures

While motivation in the American culture derives from a tradition of self-reliance and short-term success in an achievement-oriented society (to use the words of social psychologist David McClelland), other cultures illustrate different nuances of similar kinds of motives for action (McClelland 1967). In Kenya, for example, some education and a sense of status deprivation or perceived social handicap leads to innovative entrepreneurship as a way of changing the world in order not to have to change oneself. Blocked from upper-level elite positions in society, the entrepreneurs of Kenya typically found one or more small businesses, are reluctant to delegate authority and are often undone by the very diffusion of the enterprises they create (Marris 1974: 104-23). Throughout Africa, women often emerge as entrepreneurs from being the barter-traders in the marketplace who then seek to find some autonomy in a small business: this is one reason why the World Bank targets female entrepreneurs in Africa for priority support.

In Japan, creativity is approached by indirection, by recycling of old ideas in innovative ways. The Japanese cycle of creativity has been broken down into five elements that feed into each other: recycling, search, nurturing, breakthrough and refinement (Tatsuno 1990: 52-53). Tacit, informal knowledge of continuous improvement through teamwork is the Japanese way: not the Western hubris of trying to create something new under the sun, but the harmonious view of a creativity that fits in with nature and improves things subtly through new applications of existing materials and ideas.

Thus, Akihiro Yokoi, who invented *Tamagotchi*, the small electronic pet, did not come forward to claim credit for it when it became a worldwide sensation. For a year, he even let credit go to a woman at the Bandai Company where the toy was manufactured. To push forward with individualism is viewed as selfish from the traditional Japanese viewpoint. As Yokoi explained to the *New York Times* (8 March 1998): 'In Japan, we have a village society, so if someone makes a lot of money, he is alienated. There is this atmosphere that everybody should be in something together. Japanese society does not openly hail individual success.'

The Japanese do not even have their own word for entrepreneurship, except for *kigyo ka*, 'one who starts a business'. Hence, realizing their need to bring more creativity and entrepreneurship into their culture in order to compete in the emerging global economy, they have imported the English word and spend much time discussing the essence of its spirit. As David Suzuki's work has shown, the external perception of the Japanese as an homogenous culture masks a great deal of diversity, particularly in terms of how people relate to the environment. While the Japanese have an amazing ability to build on the momentum generated from elsewhere, their rapid adaptations and reactivity often demonstrate an extraordinarily subtle aesthetic touch that can be as individualistic as the Zen painting of a sitting Buddhist monk experiencing the thunderbolt of life. Or, as Zen master Yün-men put it, 'In walking, just walk. In sitting, just sit. Above all, don't wobble.'

German creativity evolves from a context of duty to the existing social order. While radical film directors such as Fassbinder may have looked at this order critically, they do not leave it behind but look at it through different colors or from a unique slant. Or, consider the dwarf's skewed perspective of the social order in Günter Grass's novel, *The Tin Drum*. Or in Nietzsche's summary in *Skirmishes in a War with the Age*: 'Liberal institutions straightway cease from being liberal the moment they are soundly established; once this is attained no more grievous and more thorough enemies of freedom exist than liberal institutions' (Nietzsche 1968: 11). The German sense of order was made explicit in a summary of the ideal German value formula by David McClelland: 'I must be able to believe and do what I should for the good of the whole' (McClelland 1964: 245-55).

Germans may critique the schema of order, but they rarely leave it behind, just as the Japanese entrepreneur knows that, in the Japanese cultural context, 'the nail that sticks up gets hit' and teamwork is the preferred avenue for innovation. As a result, young Germans are more inclined to position themselves for a niche in an established company or order than they are to start out from scratch and create their own new business. The costs of reunification in terms of cutbacks in the welfare state may be transforming these motivations (as the young realize they must create private nest eggs to safeguard retirement), encouraged by the increasing popularity of the *idea* of entrepreneurship coming from the United States. But the traditional political, cultural and educational orders are slow in adapting to such flickering interests in entrepreneurial creativity (see Chapter 3).

What creative entrepreneurs in all of these cultures tend to have in common is a sense of being something of an 'outsider', on the boundaries of the culture. Indeed, they are often either foreigners or first-generation arrivals in their cultures or else former aristocrats or elites who have been declassed and want to recover their status, like the Samurai in Japan or the Balinese aristocracy. They possess a target-oriented free-rider mentality with some sense of distance from conventional norms and routines, but nevertheless aim for conventional rewards, which they want to obtain fast, showing impatience with traditional methods and with working for others. For example, an Asian immigrant bid $175,000 for a taxi medallion (license) in order to drive his own cab in New York City in 1996. This will enable him to earn about $30,000 a year working 70 hours a week. He said, 'I want to drive for me. No more work for someone else' (*International Herald Tribune*, 21 November 1996). The American Dream is to be one's own free-rider: independent, self-reliant, the owner of one's own means of production. But, ultimately, the free entrepreneurial spirit depends on perception: the critical motivational edge that moves one to seek out a concrete way of taking risks in order to create a world of one's own.

B. The Logic of Perception

The differentiation between cultures in terms of distinctive schemata and ways of viewing entrepreneurship is an outgrowth of collective perception and socialization within cultural communities. The logic of perception, in turn, can be illustrated by what creativity consultant Edward De Bono has called 'flow-scapes': perceptual mappings of a particular theme or problem at any one moment in time that permit one to see the points of concentration in one's thinking and the interaction with less important elements. De Bono calls the empirically verifiable logic of things 'rock logic', and the unverifiable logic of perception which serves as the basis of most of our thinking and action 'water logic' (De Bono 1990).

1. De Bono's Theorem

De Bono accepts the findings of natural scientists that the brain is a self-organizing system in which a finite number of nerve states always organize themselves into a stable condition. Under any given set of circumstances, it is further assumed that a state will 'lead to' or 'be succeeded by' one other particular state. Specifically, if one draws a random set of circles on a sheet of paper and connects them up randomly with at least two lines to each circle, putting a double slash on one line leaving the circle and a single line on the other line leaving the circle, one ends up with a stable loop by entering the system at any circle and following a path such that you always exit from a circle along the line with a double slash; or, if you enter a circle from a line with a double slash, you must exit from a circle with a line with a single slash. In all cases, a stable repeating loop emerges and all other states are unstable and feed into this loop.

The key assumption of 'water logic' is that stronger elements of perception always 'flow to' or 'lead to' more dependent elements, much as water flows down a hill seeking the paths of least resistance and dwells in the deepest sink points. De Bono maintains that 'The way the brain is organized makes it *inevitable* that stable perceptions will form whatever the input.' His theorem states that 'From any input a system with a finite number of stable states and a tiring factor will always reach a stable repeating pattern' (De Bono 1994: 46 [emphasis original]).

2. Flowscapes: How they Work

In order to operationalize this theorem into 'flowscapes' or concrete pictures of our inner world of thinking, De Bono gives a simple series of steps which anyone can go through in about ten minutes (De Bono 1994: 61-69). These steps to making a flowscape can be summarized as follows:

- ☐ First, decide on the theme or problem about which you want to 'see your thinking' or illustrate in your flowscape.

- ☐ Second, make a 'stream-of-consciousness list' of all items or elements that come to mind when you think about this problem or theme or concept (typically ten or more elements or short ideas or concepts might come to mind—ideas that are spontaneous and natural, not studied nor based on 'what I *should* think').

- ☐ Third, label each of these ideas or items which are randomly listed on the stream of consciousness list with letters from the alphabet: 'A' through, for instance, 'F', just before the item or idea, using a different letter to represent each item.

☐ Fourth, considering each item one at a time, ask to which other (*single*) item on the list it naturally 'flows' or 'leads to'. This is not a question of cause and effect ('rock logic'), but merely an answer to the question 'What comes to mind next?'

☐ Fifth, label by letter on the right hand which item each item most naturally seems to 'lead' or 'flow to', so that each item leads to one other (and sometimes the same other) item. If more than one item leads to the same destination, this becomes what De Bono calls a 'collector point', an item of particular importance when later one considers the implications of one's thinking.

☐ Sixth, put down each letter *only once* on a piece of paper that now becomes the flowscape and draw arrows from each item to the items you have labeled as the destination item to which it naturally leads. Clean up and redraw the flowscape if it is messy. If you have followed the directions correctly, the flowscape should have at least one stable loop, or unbroken chain of two or more elements that lead to one another. This constitutes an endlessly repeating loop, the basis of the stability of perception (or what some might pejoratively call a 'rut' or 'hang-up'—such as, hard work leads to high income leads to heavy consumption leads to hard work).

As an illustration, consider the flowscape of 'utopia' in Figure 4, created by Fred Danback, a student at Pace University in New York. Danback was socialized in an international management seminar for which he did the flowscape and realized that, in order to create ideal environmental guidelines for entrepreneurial businesses, one must necessarily have an assumption of utopia in mind, consciously or subconsciously (Mannheim 1936).

From the 'utopia flowscape' in Figure 4, one notes the importance of building what is called 'social capital' for the sake of

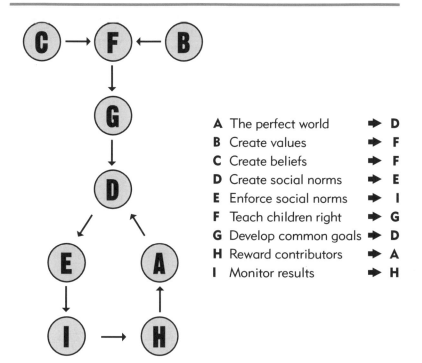

A The perfect world	➤	**D**
B Create values	➤	**F**
C Create beliefs	➤	**F**
D Create social norms	➤	**E**
E Enforce social norms	➤	**I**
F Teach children right	➤	**G**
G Develop common goals	➤	**D**
H Reward contributors	➤	**A**
I Monitor results	➤	**H**

Figure 4: **Utopia Flowscape**

Source: F. Danback

any utopian vision of an environmentally sound society. Social capital can be defined as the embedded community trust, norms and networks that facilitate collective learning and the accurate targeting of local entrepreneurship (Isaak 1995: 69; Putnam 1993: 35-42). Specifically, in the flowscape the need to create and enforce social norms and to teach social ethics to children makes it possible to cultivate an enforceable value framework. 'Teaching children right' and 'creating social norms' are the *collector points*. The *stable loop* flows from 'creating social norms' to 'enforcing social norms' to 'monitoring results' to 'rewarding contributors' to 'the perfect world', which in turn leads to 'creating social norms'.

Of course, if all of this seems too simple, it probably is. But this very simplicity, which is somewhat similar to what phenomenologists called 'bracketing out', can also be a strength and motivate us in an era of rapid change and complex information overload to have the courage to look at our own perceptions clearly in a mirror.

Water logic is just one dimension of the logic of appearances in everyday life. In this context, De Bono's flowscape approach to creative thinking is simply 'Heidegger light' or a simplistic version of past and future combining into present being in time. But the very simplicity of De Bono's flowscapes permits us to sketch out our perceptions of a topic at the moment without making too much to-do about it, to know where we stand, where our perceptions lead and what, if anything, we might want to do to shift our stable loops in more fruitful directions. In short, the virtue of the limitations of flowscapes is that they are clearly *arbitrary* with no pretense to empirically verifiable grounding. They demonstrate in no uncertain terms how far we are from truly knowing things in themselves (Kant's *Dinge an sich*). Yet our behavior is based on these arbitrary clusters of perceptions. Our collective behavior is but a constellation of such perceptual clusters or schemata over time. To change or steer these schemata requires that we are able to stand back and to examine them from a distance, to see which creative reorganizations of our perceptions might lead to breakthroughs in thinking and in solving problems. The simplicity of De Bono's perceptual maps makes them a vehicle of creativity in their own right, a method for transcending cultural biases for a moment in order to visualize where we stand on an issue.

But how can creativity or perceptual mapping be steered into designing new products or new businesses, particularly those that qualify as 'sustainable entrepreneurship?'

C. The Logic of Creative Green Design

The logic of creative green design begins with a simple assumption: pretend that *everywhere you live and work on the earth is home*. Generally, you treat your own home with care. This assumption goes against the interpretation of globalization that implies no place is really home since you are really always en route to some other place—alienating you from any place in particular, cutting you off from any roots.

If every place is home, let us further assume that you are always expecting guests: they just drop in unannounced. *So the design must not only be carefully ordered but must have an automatic cleaning-up device built in to maintain the order once established.* These two assumptions mean that you do not expect to be able to dump unwanted trash on any next-door property as a free-rider, for that property is 'home' too. *Everything that can possibly be re-used is recycled. What cannot be recycled must be processed in the least harmful way in order to keep the home on earth clean, aesthetic, healthy and in ecological balance.*

These assumptions are simple enough. But, as we shall see, their consequences can be 'radical' in the original sense of going back to 'the roots'.

The main assumption—'Earth as Home'—encourages us to create light, stable, transparent structures that are easy and efficient to maintain and simple to fix. *The chief virtue of earth as home base, as our 'maintenance base', is efficiency: cutting costs and reducing risks* (see Fig. 4).

But what happens to free-riding entrepreneurship and creativity given these assumptions? Do not these principles seem hopelessly conservative, stability-oriented, limited to the domestic and the mundane?

Not necessarily.

Freedom, entrepreneurship and creativity are alive and well—and even more satisfying in the long run for being better grounded. Rather than starting from freedom, green design starts from responsibility: the responsibility of keeping the earth in good order as our home base. We take targeted entrepreneurial risks from the home base in terms of outside markets, but we always come home again, to some home or other on the earth, with which we want to identify.

Globalization tells us we cannot go home again.

Green logic tells us that we must.

1. Steps to Creative Design

a Brainstorm: in a group of two or more. Put some (green) parameters on the table (every tennis game needs a net). In which sector, product line or product do you wish to compete? How can you minimize the energy use to almost zero? (Deliberately set an extreme that can never be met to see what wild ideas might come to help you out.) Have each person in the group write down all ideas that come to mind when 'the challenge' is presented on a slip of paper: for example, a heating system that uses no energy.

b Have one person consolidate the ideas from the slips of paper on the board or on one master list, combining similar ideas into one element or phrase.

c Have everyone in the group agree to order the items roughly into priority in terms of importance if one were to create an actual product.

d Brainstorm again out loud suggesting every possible wild product that might fit the list or some of the list. Have a group leader write down these products.

e Select one of these products at a time and have everyone in the group pretend to be an animal that would be most likely to bring the product into existence with minimal energy or resource use. For example, if the product is a household heater with least energy, pretend to be a polar bear: actually walk around and feel how it would be to have polar bear skin or movements. A new idea for insulation or for room heating as a giant sleeping bag might emerge, for example. What is the laziest man's heater you can think of? What about the most active woman's heater (using the movement of the body as one source of energy).

f Imagine how close (or far) you can get the product from the sun as a source of energy or heat or light: for example, windows designed as huge magnifying glasses?

g Once the group has come to agreement on one or more trial product ideas, imagine how this product could be adapted or used in the most extreme climates on the earth: in the desert, on a glacier, underneath the sea, a thousand feet up in the air.

h Now imagine how it could be adapted to be purchased by the poorest people on earth. The richest?

i Now imagine miniaturizing it to the smallest possible size. Blowing it up to grotesque giant size?

j Play with different colors or formats to make it light, fun, transparent, functional.

k Conceive of all possible materials that might be used to make the product. Include the most outrageous: recall the paper bathing suits sold in some hotels good for one or two swims only. Which materials are most earth friendly?

l Consider the most competitive product in this field. Imagine taking it apart. Or take it apart. Re-engineer it as Picasso would a woman's face, keeping its essential competitive elements but giving it originality and distinctiveness (e.g. the VW Beetle).

m Imagine how the product could be produced by using labor or processes that might otherwise pollute the environment (strategic deterrence). Focus on how this wild outsourcing could be used to obtain free publicity for the product. Could you create a moral crusade with it? (How about pricing it so that 10% goes to indigenous tribes?)

n Last but not least, how might the materials used to make the product be recycled in the most cost- and time-efficient way? Can you substitute for any parts or materials that do not seem easily recyclable? Are there existing public services or infrastructures that you can 'free-ride' on in order to keep costs down and to make recycling easier? Can, for example, some of the recycling process be divided up into 'green public service' jobs that the government might offer to help bring down the unemployment rate and to get people off welfare? What about recycling processes as suggested training sites or experiments to raise consciousness in public schools? Can transport costs be reduced to zero by local sourcing and personal recycling in which customers come in for refills?

In staying close to the earth, creative green design can even become easier than just any design and more sharply targeted for having a few parameters. Since the earth is home, all business designs can be as global as desired as long as they are socially and environmentally responsible in terms of their headquarters or maintenance base. Creativity is stimulated by imagining extreme cases: zero energy use, 100% recycling, maximum use of sunlight, zero cost and zero defect targets. Recall Sisyphus, the crafty and avaricious king of Corinth, who was condemned in Hades to roll a huge stone up a hill, but the stone constantly rolled back. As novelist Albert Camus put it in *The Myth of Sisyphus* (Camus 1990), although Sisyphus has been given an eternal task that is impossible in terms of pushing the stone once and for all to the top, one must imagine Sisyphus as happy in the process of his work. As we shall see in the following examples of green entrepreneurship, the very impossibility of the ideal of maintaining a pristine earth for future generations can, in itself, be the ultimate creative motivator in trying to achieve it: business, all at once, becomes the most honorable profession again as it is driven by social conscience and environmental duty in a pragmatic, innovative field that awakens collective responsiveness and claims the high moral ground. A 'utopian' vision or impulse usually propels these activities which optimistically assume a long-term 'win–win' situation—simultaneously profiting the firm financially and society in terms of increased sustainability.

2. System-Transforming Illustrations

Green entrepreneurs tend to be transparent not only about their ideals, but about their failures to measure up to them. The outdoor clothing company Patagonia Inc., for example, was the first apparel maker to sell warm-up pants made from recycled soda bottles. One of its main problems, however, is that it relies on waterproof coatings such as Gore-Tex that contain chemical toxins and bright dyes derived from strip-mined metals. In its fall 1997 catalogue, the company apologized for its use of such 'dirty' processes, arguing that to date only by using these materials can customers receive 'bombproof' outdoor clothing and the bright colors they want. Since only 20% of their customers buy the products merely because they are from an environmentally responsible firm, they have to give the customers what they want while continually pushing the limits of environmental technology. As Yvon Chouinard, Patagonia's President, told the firm's suppliers in 1996, 'We want it all. The best quality and the lowest environmental impact' (*Business Week*, 24 November 1997). What is striking is the unwillingness of Patagonia to back down from the company's environmental ideals and transparency in pointing out its limits. Only such open transparent leadership is system-transforming in moving the market and business community towards sustainable development.

a. The Body Shop

System-transforming businesses are by definition counter-cultural: either through new technological innovations or through radical social and environmental missions (or both), they view business as an ongoing experiment for which profits, although important, are secondary. Anita Roddick, founder of The Body Shop, is quite explicit: 'The way we work is quite simple. We run in the opposite direction to the rest of the cosmetics industry.' She opens her book, *Body and Soul* (Roddick 1991), with the words,

I hate the beauty business. It is a monster industry selling unattainable dreams. It lies. It cheats. It exploits women. Its major product lines are packaging and garbage. It is no wonder that Elizabeth Arden once said that the cosmetics business was the 'nastiest in the world'.

After something of a British hippy youth spent backpacking about the world (reflecting on Baudelaire's view of the fear of home and hearth as *la grande maladie*), Anita Roddick settled in (more than down) with a fellow hippy husband and two children, and began a series of start-ups from a bed-and-breakfast to a hotel to a restaurant. Social responsibility in business began with the restaurant when Roddick's husband would write the latest outrages of the city council at the top of the board on which the day's meals were scrawled. Entrepreneurship grew out of a view of life as an ongoing adventure, a counter-culture odyssey that required work as well as love to keep the expenses paid.

The actual inspiration for The Body Shop came out of Roddick's irritation at not being able to buy cosmetics by weight or bulk, like other groceries, in various sizes without overpaying for the bottle or wrappings which were unimportant to the product itself. Her knapsack travels abroad led her to discover twelve natural ingredients that women in developing countries used to keep their skin as 'smooth as silk'—in Tahiti, for example. She decided to make body creams and shampoos out of these natural ingredients and call her little shop 'The Body Shop' after auto repair businesses she had observed in California. Her husband, who was about to leave for two years to ride a horse from Buenos Aires to New York, helped her draw up a business plan after the bank turned her down for a loan when she appeared the first time with just hippy dress and enthusiasm.

The vital collateral for the loan was the old hotel that they owned, lived in and ran on the side. Roddick's motive was survival while her husband was gone. The location of the shop was carefully selected in downtown Brighton, England. It was decorated from 'Second World War mentality (shortages, utility goods, rationing) out of sheer necessity' since she had no money. The walls were painted green just because that was the only color that would cover water damage. Similar savings motives led to handwritten labels and postcards identifying the natural ingredients in the bottles. A lawyer for two funeral parlors nearby tried to stop the shop from opening for fear that clients would not want to hire a funeral director whose location was too close to a 'Body Shop'. This crisis led to Roddick's discovery that she never needed to pay a penny for advertising: she made an anonymous call about a poor defenseless woman who was being harassed by a 'mafia' of undertakers from opening a business just to feed her two children while her husband rode across South America on a horse. The paper gave her a center-page spread.

Roddick had an exceptional gift at marketing, in addition to a lifetime habit of hard work and a socially committed and flexible imagination. Necessity was always the mother of invention: no packaging, natural ingredients, no advertising and returnable bottles were cheap means to keep to a shoestring budget. For example, since perfumes were too expensive to put in the products, she filled a typesetter's tray with a choice of perfume oils and customers could choose their own fragrance to mix with whatever product they were buying. A hyper-efficient maintenance base made the entrepreneurial risk-taking distinctive and fruitful. Aesthetics, marketing and a passion for explaining what went into her natural products drove Roddick more than accounting or business knowledge.

Roddick's 'green logic' grew out of an opportunistic interpretation of social responsibility in business: a 'caring capitalism' in which businesses would 'give something back' to the communities in which they operated. She met a lot of lonely old people in her shop and targeted more of her products for them, knowing well that demographic trends pointed to an aging population. The growth area of her business was in skin care products and she knew that such products can do nothing more than cleanse, polish and protect the skin and hair and said so with few promises. The hype, therefore, had to come from describing the natural ingredients and social causes involved in the sourcing of these ingredients.

As The Body Shop expanded into more shops, fair trade became the principle: avoiding the direct exploitation of humans and animals and their habitats. This 'Trade not Aid' policy set up direct trading links with producers in developing countries in order to permit social development and environmental protection to go hand in hand. To avoid changing the native culture, Body Shop representatives sit down with members of the local community for a year and ask how they can help make the lives of the natives easier. While not denigrating humanitarian aid, the assumption is that fair trade is the only viable strategy for sustainable development in developing countries. For example, in Altamira, Brazil, the Kayapo natives worked out an arrangement with The Body Shop in which they would gather nuts, grind, cook and squash them until oil would come through that could be used as an ingredient in a hair conditioner. These activities which add value to mere nut collection permitted the Kayapo to raise the price from $8 a kilo to $38 a kilo, giving them the basis for independent dental, cultural and health programs and enabling them to survive without depending on logging and mining. As a social contribution, The Body Shop went to Nepal where the government had prohibited cutting down any more trees and taught the people how to make paper from water hyacinths, an abundant weed there. The resulting income covered child care facilities, eye care, inoculation, free food, free day care and free education for 150 people.

By the 1990s, The Body Shop had initiated a product stewardship program to embrace the ecological ethics of conventional suppliers and the environmental impact of its products from cradle to grave. The company also uses a purchasing policy and environmental checklist for all purchases from computers to company cars. And it uses a comprehensive ecological life-cycle analysis (LCA) scheme that examines inputs and outputs from manufacturing, energy, raw materials, and wastes—even assessing the potential impacts of raw materials sourcing on biodiversity, human and animal rights and endangered species. Anita Roddick summarized her vision: 'My dream for The Body Shop is to put back into the earth more than we take out.'

b. Ben and Jerry's

Just as Anita Roddick converted hippy world travel and a counter-culture lifestyle into a pragmatic, socially and environmentally responsible business success (aiming for 2,000 stores worldwide by 2000), so did Benjamin Cohen become a social missionary (together with Jerry Greenfield), going from unemployment to a social workaholic's dream business in environmentally friendly natural ice cream. Investing $12,000 in an abandoned gas station in Burlington, Vermont, in 1978, Ben and Jerry created a home-made ice cream business that would grow to a $155 million publicly owned company by the mid-1990s, represented not only in the United States and Canada, but in Great Britain, France, Israel and Russia. More importantly, the firm became known worldwide for its social responsibility, innovation and progressive activism. And the main Ben and Jerry's ice-cream factory in Waterbury became the number one tourist attraction in Vermont.

While one of Ben's intermittent jobs was to sell ice cream out of a Pied Piper ice-cream truck, the only formal training he and Jerry had in ice cream was a correspondence course from Pennsylvania State University in ice-cream making for a tuition cost of $5 (which they split). Rejecting the idea of a bagel business when they discovered how expensive the equipment was to make the bagels, they settled on ice cream, assuming the manufacturing process would be cheaper. Like Anita Roddick and her husband, Ben and Jerry found 'cheap' to have a user-friendly sound to it for someone starting up a business with little capital (a variation of the free-rider motive). And down-to-earth thrift helped to distinguish them with a provisional, 'funky' business style which appealed to everyday folks. Yet, in 1981, *Time Magazine* declared Ben and Jerry's to be 'the best ice-cream in the world', and, by the early 1990s, the company had 36% of the US 'super premium ice cream' market share. Quality was clearly a target as much as social responsibility (mirroring a more widespread trend for companies that focus on quality management to turn subsequently to environmental management).

Ben and Jerry's often epitomizes the concept of business as 'celebration'—an offspring of the hippy ' happenings' of the 1960s. Jerry's motto, 'If it's not fun, why do it?', is combined with Ben's motto, 'Business has a responsibility to give back to the community.' After their initial grand opening, as with The Body Shop, they tried to avoid advertising expenses. On Mother's Day they offered free ice-cream cones to mothers, women with gray hair, pictures of kids—or two cones for pregnant women. Other free cone days followed and Ben and Jerry created the 'Joy Gang' to bring happiness into work. This group organized the low-budget happenings including the 'Mark Twain Frog Jumping Competition', the 'Elvis Festival', movie festivals and 'The Penny Off Per Celsius Degree Below Zero Winter Extravaganza'.

While the sense of humor uplifted both people and market share, the social commitment was a natural outgrowth of 'win–win' imaginative thinking that comes from such an atmosphere. Some of the product lines, which combine both social responsibility and green logic, have included: 'Peace-Pops' in 1988 to promote their idea that 1% of the US military budget should go to peace; 'Rainforest Crunch' in 1989 to celebrate the twentieth Earth Day, a brand ice cream the nuts for which stem from tropical rainforests as an economic alternative to burning down the trees to create grazing land; and 'Wild Maine Blueberry' made from wild blueberries picked by an indigenous Indian tribe in Maine as a means of economically sustaining them.

The social context of Ben and Jerry's was consolidated by a policy through 1990 not to exceed a 5:1 ratio in terms of highest-paid to lowest-paid people in the company. Due to recruitment difficulties, this was changed to 7:1 and an exception was made for the chief executive officer recruited in 1994. But this is still a far cry from the 93:1 ratio which is average in American firms. Also, starting workers are paid the highest salaries in Vermont for this kind of work; 5% of pre-tax profits are shared with workers; and those in the firm can buy the company's stock at a 15% discount.

The company has a linked philosophy of sharing its success with its employees and the community with a deliberate irreverence towards traditional assumptions of how things are supposed to be done. Part of the 'Mission Statement' reads: 'To operate the Company in a way that actively recognizes the central role that business plays in the structure of society by initiating innovative ways to improve the quality of life of a broad community—local, national, and international.' Ben adamantly insisted that 7.5% of pre-tax profits of the overall company be given to social causes. Company committees are formed to decide how this money should be spent, involving all those who want to be involved. Ben and Jerry's Partnership in Harlem, New York, for example, gives a share of the profits to help a nearby drug-counseling center and homeless shelter founded by the store's owner. And, in the early 1990s, a committee decided to support the Children's Defense Fund in order to put the interest of poor children at the top of the political agenda: 70,000 postcards were sent to Congress for the cause. The profits from the Ben and Jerry's 'Scoop Shop' in Petrozavodsk, Russia, go to help finance an intercultural exchange program.

The thrust of these green businesses from the Anglo-American West—The Body Shop and Ben and Jerry's—is to start on a shoestring budget, with a strong sense of social mission, flexible imagination, a preoccupation with quality and an ultimate aim of giving back to the earth and the communities in which the businesses operate. Marketing, with a little imagination and subtle pushing of social causes along with the products, can take care of itself. It becomes what Charles Hampden-Turner called 'political marketing': customers vote when they purchase explicitly socially responsible products over socially indifferent competitors. Workers are enveloped in a sense of solidarity, equity and motivation that transcends the mere economic profit motive. Entrepreneurship becomes an all-consuming lifestyle—a good cause, good fun and a good job all wrapped into one. Customers sense the enthusiasm and community responsiveness and want to participate.

c. Spinnrad

Of course, green entrepreneurship is found elsewhere. The Germans, for instance, have a deep-seated commitment to preserve their forests and to improve the environment in the context of their social market economy. In 1970, the Spinnrad company was founded in Gelsenkirchen, Germany. The raw materials for cosmetics were provided through catalogues, and customers were asked to mix and make their own. Demand grew to the point that, in 1986, the first sales stores were established using a franchising concept under the direction of Peter and Brigitte Krämer. The sales grew from DM2.1 million in 1986 to DM126 million in 1996.

The explicit philosophy of Spinnrad is to demonstrate that a profit-oriented company can simultaneously respect the environment and work towards being socially responsible. Instead, for example, of offering merely throw-away containers, the company provides containers that can be refilled for many products (shampoo and shower gel, for example). In order to limit the amount of packaging waste in their 'Frusip's drinks', they offer them in a highly concentrated form. They sell tea and coffee from the 'TransFair' brand, which has as its goal the generation of a fair income for the peasant families of developing countries. Their 'Cafe Foresta' brand of coffee supports small farmer cooperatives high in the mountains of Costa Rica with an integrated regional program to help protect the rainforest.

Spinnrad avoids excess packaging wherever possible and is developing its management system to harmonize with the European Union's Eco-audit Order 1836/93—the Environmental Management and Audit Scheme (EMAS) (see Chapter 4). Since many of the firm's products are based on coconut oil, for every kilo of coconut oil used an additional 50% is allocated for the financial sake of the Evangelical Church of Westphalia, which, in turn, uses the money to improve the living conditions of the coconut farmers in the Philippines. Last but not least, Spinnrad cooperates with the BUND (*Bund für Umwelt und Naturschutz*), the organization for the protection of the environment and nature in Germany. By 1990, Spinnrad was exporting to Belgium, Denmark, the Netherlands, Austria, Switzerland and Hungary. And, by 1994, the company had 117 stores and opened an office in Ho-Chi-Minh City in Vietnam, which served as the source for rattan and gumtree wood used in the new store design for the franchises.

A clear pattern emerges in the evolution of ecopreneurship: when a green start-up begins in a developed country, as the firm internationalizes, it takes root in developing or emerging economies on a basis that is not just for profit but which aims for trade, not aid. However, not all green start-ups are initiated in developed countries.

d. The Honey Bee Network

In 1993 Professor Anil Gupta of the Indian Institute of Management founded the Society for Research and Initiatives for Sustainable Technologies and Institutions (SRISTI) in Ahmedabad, India. This is a non-governmental organization (NGO) that aims 'to strengthen the capacity of grassroots inventors, innovators and ecopreneurs engaged in conserving biodiversity and developing eco-friendly solutions to local problems.' The key focus of this green NGO is 'The Honey Bee', a newsletter and information network in six languages dealing with examples of local ecopreneurship. The organisation's website can be found at *http://csf.colorado.edu/sristi*.

Honey Bee represents a philosophy of authentic discourse which strives to be accountable and fair. The honey bee 'collects pollen without impoverishing the flowers, and it connects flower to flower through pollination'. In terms of our society: when we collect knowledge from people, we should ensure that people do not become poorer from sharing their insights with us. Innovators need to be connected with one another through feedback communication and networking in the local language, whatever that may be. If consultancies or other sources of income result from people's knowledge, a fair share of the income should go back to the providers in a transparent manner. And, tellingly, 'We write in the English language which connects us globally but alienates us locally.' The Honey Bee network strives to reach people from whom they have learned who normally cannot be reached. They struggle to bridge the gap between those who professionally receive recognition and the people who suffer silently, the human resources underneath the recognition. Their central concern is the ethics of knowledge extraction. The network is a catalyst for a global movement to conserve biodiversity through documentation, experimentation, value-addition and dissemination of local innovations by farmers, pastoralists, artisans and horticulturists. A significant focus is on the protection of intellectual property rights of grass-roots innovators.

One of Anil Gupta's associates, Astad Pastakia, wrote a dissertation on agricultural pest management uncovering the role of grass-roots ecopreneurs as change agents for a sustainable society. 'Ecopreneurs', he writes, 'bring about change by compelling various actors in the production–consumption cycle to recognize and deal with environmental externalities' (Pastakia 1996: 1). Pastakia distinguishes between *social ecopreneurs* who use persuasive and educational tactics to influence the behavior of others, and *commercial ecopreneurs* who eliminate polluting products and processes from the market by providing consumers and investors with more eco-friendly options.

Two of the ecopreneurs interviewed harnessed the energies of the Swadhyay socio-religious movement in the western states of India—a religion that shows great respect for sentient beings and the environment—in order to overcome resistance to their herbal pesticides. Such resistance comes particularly from state regulations requiring registration based on tests on bioefficacy, toxicity and environmental effects, which are prohibitively expensive for most grass-roots entrepreneurs. However, another ecopreneur ran into the opposite problem: insufficient state regulation setting quality standards for vermicompost, making it impossible to check unscrupulous entrepreneurs from cheating customers and giving the product a bad name in a growing business sector. In this case, since farmers had to make systematic changes in their farming methods to substitute vermicompost for chemical pesticides, the resistance among potential users was high. And, if a stricter code of bioethics in natural farming was introduced as well, the resistance was the highest.

From a comparative international viewpoint, social resistance to bioethics and to the conditions of viable ecopreneurship must be explained in order to be overcome. In order to do this and to understand the optimum relationship between the government and markets for sustainability, we must turn to theories that give us a concrete sense of why human beings grow up with indifferent feelings towards the land off which they live and towards the ecological heritage they will pass on to their children and grandchildren. Such theories take us back as far as the French Revolution, which promised universalism and delivered rootlessness, and as far forward as the globalization of the twenty-first century, which threatens to become the *reducto ad absurdum* of modern mobility and indifference to any particular place for the sake of freedom and change.

Chapter 2
Eco-Theories and Government Regulation

A. Walden and the Land Ethic

People are socialized to be indifferent to the land on which they are raised. They are taught that they cannot go home again. To be modern is to be mobile, to trade roots for upward mobility. The old land lies behind. Homes are deserted as globalization transforms traditions into mere provisional cultures. Even Henry David Thoreau's 'Walden'—that utopia of utopias—satisfied the transcendentalist only two years and two months. Then he up and left the cabin built with his own hands on Walden Pond and moved on (Thoreau 1854). Americans, after all, have always been restless. Now they have helped to globalize the world on their model, making other peoples restless too. And, on the site Thoreau left behind, up to 3,000 tourists tromp through every summer day, transforming a self-sufficient home base into a global commercial attraction.

In his classic essay, 'The Land Ethic', the American theorist and father of wildlife conservation, Aldo Leopold, illustrates the indifference of people to property with a classical example:

> When god-like Odysseus returned from wars in Troy, he hanged all on one rope a dozen slave-girls of his household whom he suspected of misbehavior during his absence. This

> hanging involved no question of propriety. The girls were property. The disposal of property was then, as now, a matter of expediency, not of right and wrong (Leopold 1949).

The mobile traveler perceives women as 'property' to be disposed of as a practical matter of convenience. Similarly, land comes to be seen not as 'home' but merely as 'property' used or disposed of as is expedient for short-term commercial ends. But Leopold points out that, in the time of Odysseus, a sense of ethics did exist: the wife of Odysseus, for example, was to remain faithful twenty years. Later, as society moved on, slaves came to be regarded as persons in a community with rights and obligations. Ethics, in short, evolved to make owners responsible for community obligations in terms of property. Aldo Leopold argued that, over time, indifference to property is increasingly constrained by community obligations both to the land to others in the community. Water will no longer be regarded merely as an expedient way of floating barges or carrying off sewage; nor will plants and animals merely be seen as indifferent commodities that can be extinguished at will if it is commercially convenient. Commitment to community implies ethical limits to the freedom of action in the struggle for existence which distinguish social from antisocial behavior. The land and its biodiversity demand ethical respect as interdependent parts of the community as the ethical sense of its members evolves.

At the end of the twentieth century, for example, secondary-school children are systematically taken on field trips to give them a sense of biodiversity and the need for its maintenance in Costa Rica. With 5% of the world's biodiversity, the Costa Rican government correctly views ecology as a rich natural resource, charging multinational companies such as Merck not only for samples but for 2% of any money made on pharmaceuticals coming from these scarce resources. Other so-called 'developed' countries have not yet evolved to this stage in terms of the land ethic.

In his chapter 'Economy' in *Walden*, Thoreau argues that modern man tends to abuse the land and his own pocketbook by oversheltering: 'It is evident that the savage owns his shelter because it costs so little, while the civilized man hires his commonly because he cannot afford to own it.' Thoreau is, ultimately, a free-rider: he suggests that, in walking through rich forests owned and maintained by others and in having time to chat with his neighbors, he gets more pleasure from life than those who own too much property which they are constantly busy maintaining. If you own a cow, the cow milks you; live lightly on the land while being responsible for it and praise its natural gifts: these are the maxims of Thoreau.

> But lo! men have become the tools of their tools. The man who independently plucked the fruits when he was hungry is become a farmer; and he who stood under a tree for shelter, a housekeeper. We now no longer camp as for a night, but have settled down on earth and forgotten heaven.

The shrewd traveller visits someone else's summer house, catching enjoyment on the fly while saving the cost of maintenance. The wise walker in a large city such as London or Manhattan schedules an extra 'buffer' hour between appointments in order to have time to look up and see the sky between the buildings.

Thoreau continues:

> We have built for this world a family mansion, and for the next a family tomb. The best works of art are the expression of man's struggle to free himself from this condition, but the effect of our art is merely to make this low state comfortable and that higher state to be forgotten.

The maxims to be drawn here are clear. Under-house. Collect fewer things. Transcend the mundane. Thoreau went to jail rather than pay taxes. He was a free-rider with principles, vision, and a sense of the lightness of being.

But his heritage presents us with a problem. We have a capitalist global economy that thrives on accumulation. Americans all want their individual Waldens—to *own*. They call this the 'American Dream'. And they are busily exporting this vision worldwide through 'privatization'—the ideological siren call for the sake of economic growth, job creation and more accumulation. To the extent that twenty-first-century individuals live by capitalism and yet believe in Thoreau, they want to eat their cake and have it too: they want to own property while free-riding upon it. They want as much individual advantage with as little individual responsibility as possible. We call this mobility and flexibility in the markets. Land becomes mere property: a provisional, commercial thing.

American poet and farmer Wendell Berry laments the loss of local culture in the rootless commercialization of land in his essay 'The Work of Local Culture' (Berry 1990):

> As local community decays along with local economy, a vast amnesia settles over the countryside. As the exposed and disregarded soil departs with the rains, so local knowledge and local memory move away to the cities or are forgotten under the influence of homogenized salestalk, entertainment, and education.

Globalization is the ultimate form of amnesia in terms of the land ethic. We can always travel to some other place and ditch our local responsibilities and the mess we have left behind. We are global free-riders, mentally rootless on the Internet, physically restless, shifting jobs, homes, countries, comfortably forgetting interrelationships with people and place. We are the universal forgetters of principle. Freedom is all. Our favorite river is the River Lethe.

B. Deep Ecology and Speciesism

Aldo Leopold can be called the father of 'deep ecology' in urging us all to learn to 'think like a mountain' (Leopold 1969). Human chauvinism is put on the back burner. The celebration of nature and the land ethic become the prime movers of thought and action.

Inspired by the Norwegian philosopher Arne Naess, American ecologist Bill Devall proposed the term 'deep ecology' (Devall 1980) to designate a revolutionary movement seeking a new metaphysics, epistemology, cosmology and environmental ethics of the person/planet as distinct from mere environmental reformism. Environmental reformism, according to Devall, merely seeks to control some of the work of the air and water pollution and inefficient land use policies of industrialized nations and to rescue a few 'designated wilderness areas' before the wilderness disappears.

Deep ecology helped to give birth to a number of political movements and ideologies: Greenpeace, Earth First, the Sierra Club, and green parties of various shades. It is illustrated in the arguments of Professor Christopher Stone for the legal status of trees and valleys in a trial the Sierra Club brought in the 1970s against Walt Disney Corporation, which was planning to develop the wild valley of Mineral King in California (Stone 1974). Although the legal appeal lost, three judges voted for it, siding with the rights of natural objects in the environment over mere human, corporate claims. But North American law resists such claims, in general, since it seeks to award claims to identifiable interests. For example, a Law Reform Commission of Canada in 1985 concluded that 'The scope of a Criminal Code offense against the environment should not extend to protecting the environment for its own sake apart from human values, rights and interests.' The deep ecology movement, not to mention 'the environment for its own sake', is in deep trouble in an era of globalization dominated by the spread of North American and British 'interest' ideology worldwide.

Part of the problem is the etymology of the word 'environment' itself, which (according to *Webster's Dictionary*) means 'surroundings': that is 'the aggregate of all the external conditions and influences affecting the life and development of an organism, specifically, the human organism and human society'. 'Environment' is, from the outset, declassed, a mere periphery, having no significance if not related to human interests or needs 'inside' it. The deep ecology movement constitutes a massive protest against this taking of the environment for granted and putting the interests of the human animal before all else.

Philosophers Arne Naess and George Sessions identified a number of key principles of deep ecology, including the following: (1) human and non-human life have intrinsic value in themselves and have the right to flourish independent of the usefulness of the non-human world for human purposes; (2) the diversity and richness of life-forms have value in themselves; (3) except to satisfy vital needs, humans have no right to reduce this diversity; (4) a substantial decrease in the human population will not harm the flourishing of human life and culture and is essential for the flourishing of non-human life; (5) humans interfere with the non-human world excessively and the situation is deteriorating rapidly; and (6) an ideological shift towards appreciating life quality over an increasingly higher standard of living is overdue, with requisite changes in government policy (Naess 1986; Sessions 1987).

The ideological shift called for by the deep ecologists constitutes a reversal of the French Revolution's Declaration of the Rights of Man and of the Citizen, which defined liberty as 'being unrestrained in doing anything that does not interfere with another's rights'. Freedom above all else. Humans shape the world in their own interests, according to their whims: the human as the ultimate free-rider! In contrast, deep ecologists ask that the whole be treated as more important than the parts, that biodiversity take priority, not homocentrism. Humans should be in their proper place in the natural universe, not the be-alls and end-alls. Biodiversity must become more than a safety valve for human utility. The rainforest is not just fodder for someone's chainsaw.

Deep ecology is essentially a counter-culture movement, a movement that counters the Cartesian culture of the West, which splits mind from body, humans from nature, subject from object. In *Le contrat naturel* (1990), Michael Serres, for example, calls for a return to nature and asks humankind to leave behind the *parasitic* relationship of mastery and possession in favor of a *symbiotic* relationship of appreciative listening: a 'natural contract' of reciprocity. Serres is concerned that, for the first time in the history of humanity, the problems involving the destruction of the earth have become global; the disenchantment of nature via the applied rationality of industrialism has reached an extreme. Humans must give back to nature the status of 'legal subject' and return some of what has been taken.

In Germany, Professors Malte Faber, Reiner Manstetten and John Proops look at deep ecology in terms of the purpose or *telos* of organisms. They discover three *tele* (intentional purposes) for organisms: (1) self-maintenance, development and self-realization; (2) replication and renewal; and (3) service to other organisms, to other species or the whole of nature (Faber *et al.* 1995). They maintain that the sustainability of an ecosystem requires a balance and harmony between these mutually supporting *tele* or purposes. Like Aristotle, who found the *telos* of the oak tree to exist in the potential of the acorn, they find the intentionality of developed organisms to lie in these three basic kinds of *tele* or purposes. Presumably, the highest level of development of living organisms is indicated by the maintenance and flourishing of the whole of nature. Clearly, according to this standard, a majority of human beings have a way to go yet in their development.

The difficulty with this form of analysis is the teleological fallacy: the implicit assumption that, given the seed or *telos*, the organisms will inevitably develop to their full potential rather than, for example, self-destructing. What if, for example, human organisms are pre-programmed more for competitive one-upmanship than for cooperation and strive more to outposition other groups economically and militarily—through nuclear proliferation, for instance—than sustain peace and stability among all living beings? For every *telos* full of the light of the acorn, there may be a dark *telos*, the Faustian pride of technological and economic development over everything else (which Faber and Manstetten, to their credit, have pointed out in their lectures). We are somehow left with the eternal conflict of Manichean forces of lightness and dark, which have led some to despair of the human animal and to take up the cause of defending the priority rights of other species.

The Logic of Animal Liberation

These schools of thought range from the animal liberation movement to 'antispeciesism' ('speciesism' refers to the bias in favor of one's own species and against those of members of other species). Animal liberation emerged as a reaction against the praise of the doubting human mind (*cogito*) of Descartes, which rendered all other animal species to the status of mere machines.

'Man thinking'—so well captured in the famous statue by Rodin—abstracts human value from bodily functions and environment alike. In this sense, Cartesianism can be viewed as a kind of intellectual romanticism: one mind takes on the universe. The ability to think, to doubt, to speak these thoughts—these cognitive functions are what distinguish the human animal. And the implicit assumption is the more *cogito*, the better; the more human thinking, the better.

The existentialists already rebelled against Descartes's 'I think therefore I am' logo of human significance. Miguel de Unamuno, for example, turned the phrase literally on its head: 'I am therefore I think.' Existence precedes essence. Physical being, feeling, instinct—all too much conditioned by the environment—before mere thought.

Has not the hubris of cognition led to the splitting of the atom, resulting in the atomic bomb and nuclear proliferation? Has not intellectual romanticism resulted in a binary binge of computer development and technology that the human mind can hardly keep up with, not to mention information overload resulting in 'data smog' or pollution (in David Schenk's words; Schenk 1997) and culturally induced attention deficit disorders? For example, while in 1971 the average American was targeted by 560 daily advertising messages, two decades later the number was up to 3,000 messages per day—a sixfold increase. The value of too much *cogito* (too much cognition or doubting) must, itself, be doubted—particularly when the effect is to satiate the world with more information, technology and economic development than can be can coped with. We are, after all, human *animals*.

Since only the human species has developed the technological capacity to eliminate all other species, the 'speciesism' involved in human pride must be balanced by something else for the sake of sustainability. This observation leads us to the troubling arguments of animal liberationists such as Australian philosopher Peter Singer. Singer (1991) points to the evidence that non-human animals can suffer and that there is no moral justification for assuming that the suffering of non-human animals is of a lesser moral status than the suffering of human animals. Specifically, he begins with an assumption that few of us would question: *All human beings are equal in moral status.* But then he argues that this basic ethical principle is not compatible with the proposition of speciesism, which has come to be taken for granted by most humans: *All human beings are of superior moral status to non-human beings.* To show that these two principles many of us take for granted are not compatible, Singer takes an unusual tack. He suggests that, if we compare human beings with irreversible intellectual disabilities or brain disorders with animals of higher communicative skills (chimpanzees, for instance), then it becomes almost impossible to draw a line in terms of non-human and human. Indeed, it may be easier for us to empathize with the chimp who feels pain and can communicate it than with a human being who appears no longer neither to be able to feel nor communicate. Morally, he suggests, we are equally obligated to trouble ourselves about non-human animals who suffer as we are about humans. But we need not concern ourselves with heads of lettuce that feel nothing and therefore cannot suffer.

The modern logic of animal liberation goes beyond its own previous logic which asserted that we degrade ourselves and lose humanity when we mistreat domestic animals. And modern logic transcends the notion that, by prohibiting the mistreatment of domestic animals, humans may be socialized to treat each other without violence. Singer's logic of animal liberation goes to the extreme of asserting that non-human animals also have moral rights, if not legal rights. His logic goes back to the utilitarianism of British philosopher Jeremy Bentham, who wrote:

The day may come when the rest of the animal creation may acquire those rights which never could have been withholden from them but by the hand of tyranny . . . A full-grown horse or dog is beyond comparison a more rational, as well as a more conversable animal, than an infant of a day or a week or even a month old . . . The Question is not, Can they reason? nor Can they talk? But, Can they *suffer?'* (cited in Singer 1991).

So, according to Singer, any living thing that is capable of suffering or of happiness—capable, in short, of having interests—has formal equality. The stone a boy kicks down the road has no interests, according to Singer; but a mouse the boy might kick down the road does have interests and, therefore, has equal rights to treatment as a being capable of suffering.

Animal liberation as radical utilitarianism would therefore aim to reduce the suffering or increase the happiness of the greatest number of living beings with interests—whether human or non-human. And it logically follows that the greatest diversity of species should be sustained, each species with its own equal rights. The chauvinism of the human species stands outs in glaring disproportion to the balance of species that this vision presupposes. Hubris strikes like a stone in the lake of harmony of living, suffering creatures, spreading its ripples ever further. The question becomes: Is green logic necessarily incompatible with humanism and the Western tradition that affirms it?

C. Ecological Humanism

Rousseau and Kant both identified *freedom* as the characteristic that ultimately distinguishes human beings from other animals. Kant went on to suggest that humans alone also could conceive of immortality and God. There is no evidence that non-human animals conceive of free choice between alternatives, or make sacrifices for the sake of some vision of immortality or of service to God or gods.

In *The New Ecological Order*, French philosopher Luc Ferry (1992) stresses the continuity between the deep ecologists and animal liberationists such as Singer, pointing out that nature is seen as a continuum between human and non-human animals. Antispeciesism argues, as does anti-racism and anti-sexism, that all living things should be equal regardless of race, gender, species or origin. But freedom, in this context, the basis of ecological humanism, is *anti*-natural: human beings *decide* to go against natural urges in order to make sacrifices for something which they perceive to be greater or more significant. *Ethical* choice, in short, presupposes freedom that is a characteristic of consciousness only found in the human animal. Ferry argues that both deep ecology and animal liberation involve antihumanism: they do not mention 'culture', which is an outgrowth of freedom and involves a *separation* from nature.

Deep ecology and the utilitarianism of Singer's antispeciesism, in contrast, view everything as natural, making no allowance for the cultural distinctiveness that is the essence of humanism. Non-humans, according to Ferry, have no culture but merely customs and modes of life. Therefore, within the democratic societies of legal humanism, nature can occupy only the status of object not of subject. The opposite view—often advocated by green parties, according to Ferry—is revolutionary and involves a radical deconstruction of humanism. Moreover, designing a normative, antihumanist ethic is a contradiction in terms, since only human beings can create normative evaluative frameworks—even if these should aim to declass human activities in the overall scheme of things. And, if the biosphere were to become the only subject of the law, as the most romantic of the deep ecologists suggest, it must be recalled that nature brings death and destruction as well as life and harmony—the HIV virus, hurricanes and plague as well as rainforests, birdsong and clear blue sky. Laws are for human beings. Stones, valleys and non-human animals are objects of human law, not subjects, Ferry concludes. The temptation to raise up the rights of the non-human to the human level appears to surface because of a rejection of the consequences of modernity at a certain stage of economic development and a sense that faith in human reason alone was perhaps overrated in the twentieth century.

Modern, all too Modern

Green logic implies a longing for virgin forests lost, for a simpler pastoral past not yet overwhelmed by modern, industrialized development. 'Modern' not only implies a secularized world, but a worldliness declassed from a green perspective: 'postmodern' is 'in'; 'modern' is passé.

An inevitable historical transformation has occurred. Developing countries have mimicked the industrialized West and, as they have shifted from agricultural to industrial and service industries, a surfeit of modernity has spread throughout the world: a plethora of high-rises, flashing billboards, wired metropolises, beeping cellular phones and streets clogged with Mercedes, BMWs and CO_2-spewing sports utility vehicles. Deregulation, privatization, instant global financial, technological and communication flows have all stimulated a race toward material upward mobility measured by GNP growth and the latest in television, computer and automobile luxury. And, inevitably, as the luxuries of modernity have spread everywhere, they have started to lose their social status. Invidious distinctions can no longer be made on the basis of material trophies alone if everyone can purchase them. Thus, a postmodern reaction has set in among the educated rich in the West looking for post-industrial values, green cachet and natural oases protected from overdevelopment. *Green logic is motivated by a sense of loss not merely of environmental wholeness but of social meaning: the creature comforts of the material world alone are not enough to bring satisfaction. Green logic longs for spiritual recovery decked out in the garb of nature.*

For modernization is secularization: the systematic demotion of spiritual significance. The loss of the legitimacy of religion in modern, secular liberal societies complements the loss of legitimacy of politics. The rise of fundamentalism, of movements for regional autonomy, of cults, and the spread of social move-

ments for single issues such as the environment all are stimulated by the loss of religious and political legitimacy in the modern world. As philosopher George Santayana put it, 'The mass
of mankind is divided into two classes, the Sancho Panzas who
have a sense for reality, but no ideals, and the Don Quixotes
with a sense for ideals, but mad' (Santayana 1957). Modernity
had the effect of seeming to force everyone to become some
sort of Sancho Panza or other in order to become competitive
and to succeed economically. But, when economic success itself
becomes so widespread as to no longer be that desirable, the
repressed Don Quixotes rise to seek their moment in the sun.
Santayana proposes the expedient of recognizing facts as facts
and accepting ideals as ideals. But green logic has become so
controversial that this simple distinction often eludes the power
of human discrimination.

The spread of Western democratic liberal democracy has had
the effect of turning culture into a market commodity with a
thrust towards the lowest common denominator for the sake
of economies of scale. This massive consumerism came on top
of the rootlessness resulting from the cosmopolitanism of the
French Revolution—any citizen should be a free and equal citizen of the world. Not surprisingly, these socioeconomic trends
of lowest-common-denominator consumerism and citizenship
led to romantic, national and regional reactions against modern secularization and globalization. While green movements
were among the forces to counter mainstream development,
they ultimately had to transcend national boundaries, even if
they emerged from romantic origins aiming to protect the root-
edness of the local environment. For the Chernobyls and nuclear
tests of this world know no national boundaries. Nor do the
CO_2 emissions from sports utility vehicles and industrial sites.
Nor do the smoke, haze and atmospheric consequences stemming from rainforests set ablaze in Indonesia, Brazil or Mexico.
One strategy used to transcend the limits of national boundaries while recognizing the realities of globalization was to advocate a variation of the ideology of the market: 'free-market environmentalism'.

D. Free-Market Environmentalism

Free-riding entrepreneurs are engines of economic growth in the economist's vision of open systems. Environmentalists, on the other hand, often assume closed systems. As William Ashworth put it in *The Economy of Nature* (1995),

> Ecologists study the behavior of closed systems. This leads to a view of inputs and outputs radically different from the open systems view of the economists. Open systems imply throughput—substances coming from one place, flowing through the system, and then going out to someplace different. Closed systems imply cycles. To an ecologist the someplace that substances come from and the someplace they go are ultimately the same place.

One theory that aims to take care of this paradox of envisioning closed systems within open systems is free-market environmentalism. This vision is a variety of a neoclassical economic liberal's utopia. Free-market environmentalism, as advocated, for example, by American professors Terry Anderson and Donald Leal, assumes that the main function of government is to reduce the cost of defining and enforcing property rights, leaving solutions to environmental problems up to the efficiency of private markets (Anderson and Leal 1991).

Free-market environmentalists contrast water trades in the United States, which have enhanced environmental quality through private water institutions, with the water projects of the government Bureau of Reclamation that resulted in the damming of all the major water systems in the West and the end of hundreds of salmon and steelhead runs. They look for compatibility between market processes, good resource stewardship and environmental quality. Since survival rewards species that successfully fill a niche, they argue that owners who efficiently manage their resources are rewarded with wealth, attracting entrepreneurs to open niches. However, central planners, in contrast to flexible entrepreneurs, cannot determine which niches are open and how they should be filled, given the diffuse nature within an ecosystem.

In *Free Market Environmentalism*, Anderson and Leal celebrate micro-economic efficiency in the allocation of resources as their highest value. But, as environmental critic Mark Saghoff (1994) has noted, 'Nobody, it seems, ever went broke turning dells into delis, arcadias into arcades, or, in the words of the popular song, paradises into parking lots.' In short, there are moral, aesthetic, cultural and political values that transcend mere economic efficiency concerns when it comes to effluents, emissions and eyesores. As opposed to most environmentalists, Anderson and Leal assume the priority of satisfying preferences on a willing-to-pay basis of efficiency. As Saghoff notes, this can lead to pernicious effects if people can take what they want and need only to pay compensation after the fact. He cites the example of owners of whaling ships and merchant vessels in the early nineteenth century who would shanghai passers-by to fill out their crews, put them to work on the ships for, say, three years, and only have to pay the 'objective' salaries they deserved after the event in the courts. Polluters could similarly shanghai people and property in their region with their emissions and then just compensate their victims for minimal risks in labor or other markets at rates decided by the government or courts. The interests and health of the private property owner would no longer be protected adequately by the government.

And, as to the argument that large owners will be more responsible and efficient in managing government-owned wilderness areas if they are privatized and sold to the highest bidder, diffuse environmental groups would rightly protest that they would have a much harder time getting the cash and management together than would large oil or energy-extracting companies. The question is whether the freedom of the polluter or the polluted takes priority: a question that cannot be answered on the ground of allocative efficiency alone.

The free-market environmentalist's view of utopia is close to that of libertarian philosopher Robert Nozick's (1974) vision of a minimalist state that exists only to keep law and order and to enforce existing private property contracts. Otherwise, the state is to stay out of the way of productive entrepreneurs and people who want to make a living and stimulate economic growth. Clearly, this is a largely negative view of the state: utopia is freedom of the individual from the state with minimalist exceptions in order to protect private property. The libertarian argument for protecting the environment by preserving property rights above all else is quite different than advocating that the best way to protect property rights is to preserve the environment. The implications of this viewpoint become clearer when free-market environmentalism is contrasted with another view of the state and environmental policy—that of the social market economy.

E. Social Market Environmentalism

The most developed example of 'the social market economy' is Germany. In the German social market economy, the government assures the solidarity of the social contract through class-mitigating welfare measures (state-subsidized healthcare, pensions, unemployment and disability insurance, university tuition, labor training, environmental maintenance), while leaving the private sector free to operate in the economic market. The social 'maintenance base' is thus clearly separated from the freedom to take entrepreneurial risk.

The backdrop of consciousness of social order is important in considering whether or not individuals perceive entrepreneurship in a social context or in an asocial context. Recall that entrepreneurship is a creative variation of free-rider behavior. Indifferent as to the source of his or her funding, the entrepreneur must free-ride as much as possible in the start-up phase to survive more than five years in business. Therefore, if environmental responsibility is perceived to be a negative deterrent or a punitive set of regulations, the entrepreneur will be tempted to avoid such regulations and to free-ride on the earth in order to survive financially. If, on the other hand, environmental responsibility has become so intrinsic in the social order that it comes to define majority preferences in the market, then the entrepreneur may be more tempted to start up an environmentally responsible business in order to gain market share and to survive. The thesis here is that environmental consciousness has become such a part of the German social order today that entrepreneurs are increasingly tempted to think green in order to succeed on the market, while in the United States, the birthplace of free-market environmentalism, green choices are more legislated than intrinsic to the social order and constitute just one fashionable boutique among many for the individual consumer rather than a perceived duty of social conscience. Or, to put it another way, the threat of litigation posed by environmentalists is more of a stick than a carrot in the US, whereas recycling regulations in Germany may function more as a carrot for the development of environmental businesses than is the case in the US, where such regulations are less likely to be enforced than they are in Germany. German 'closed systemness' may foster more economic 'greenness' than American open-system assumptions.

On a European scale, the German government has attempted to lead the way in raising the environmental consciousness of all European Union member countries and to impose stiff European regulations to deter free-rider behavior by European entrepreneurs that is not friendly towards the environment. In fact, the tough German environmental regulations domestically have led large firms to create a counter-strategy of self-enforcement: all energy-intensive industries in Germany voluntarily agreed to cut emissions of CO_2 by 20% by 2000 from 1990 levels, stimulating Germany's chemical industry association to develop voluntary proposals covering a host of environmental areas (*Chemical Week*, 12 May 1994: 37-38). Moreover, German companies make up 75% of the European companies that have satisfied the criteria for and have become certified to the voluntary European Union Environmental Management and Audit Scheme (EMAS), which came into effect in April 1995 (see Chapter 3).

Green Dots and the Dual System

The 'Green Dot' waste reduction system is perhaps the clearest symbol of the closed-loop economy in Germany. As of 1991, the German Packaging Ordinance made companies responsible for their products from manufacture through to disposal—the 'user pays principle'. The aim was to avoid packaging, reduce material used and recycle unavoidable packaging. The Packaging Ordinance proposed two ways of reducing waste: either used packaging must be taken back by the retail trade or a nationwide, privately organized system has to be used for the collection, sorting and recycling of post-consumer sales packaging.

The 'Dual System' (Duales System Deutschland GmbH, founded in 1990) was responsible for putting this legislation into practice. As a result of this system, the amount of material used to produce packaging for private households and small businesses dropped by 570,000 tons from 1991 to 1993 (Rob 1996: 7). In 1995, 5.1 million tons of post-consumer sales packaging were collected, the equivalent to 79% of all sales packaging generated by private households and small businesses (*Duales System Deutschland Annual Report*, 1996). Or, in this sense, the system can be considered to be 79% 'closed'. The non-profit Dual System is financed by fees received for licensing the use of the 'green dot' displayed on products that are certified by the system. (The fees are assessed on the basis of the kind and weight of material being reprocessed.) The system in Germany has become so pervasive that most trash is pre-sorted by consumers before it is picked up! At the same time, the system is being financially undermined by free-riders—those using the logo but not paying the fees.

Ultimately, if the world market goes increasingly green through international regulations and environmental consciousness-raising, the German entrepreneur is positioned to be at the forefront of the market. An example of this would be the universal acceptance of the Earth Summit's concept of setting a 25% waste reduction goal for every major city in the world. On the other hand, if such environmental regulations and behavior are not realized, the Germans may find themselves to be on the wrong end of a variable-sum game in which most entrepreneurs will find a way to go around the regulations and to free-ride at the expense of German competitiveness.

This danger is seen domestically in the fact that, statistically, the growth of entrepreneurial small businesses is much higher among foreigners moving into Germany than it is among Germans themselves (*The Week in Germany*, 26 January 1996). And it is seen internationally in the trend of German entrepreneurial capital flowing out of the country to set up subsidiaries or businesses in countries that are less regulated—that is, almost anywhere else. Meanwhile, unemployment in Germany has hit a post-World War II high, and the leaders of all German political parties agreed that the unemployment rate must be cut by half by 2000 (but have failed to follow through in practice, partly due to the requirements of European Monetary Union). The trend in Germany appears, as in the United States, to be to deregulate the economy for the sake of economic growth, competitiveness and job creation. The difference is that, in Germany, the environmental ethic is much more internalized than it is in the US, to the point that, in the early 1990s, environmental concerns were the top German political priority in opinion polls. In 1992, for example, 67% of Germans polled were 'very worried' about global warming (the greenhouse effect) compared to only 30% in the US; and 73% of the Germans were 'very worried' about the destruction of the ozone layer compared to 43% of Americans (OECD 1992). However, later opinion polls indicated a greater concern with criminality than with environmental issues, with the problem of unemployment taking the position of the highest priority concern (helping to bring the Social Democrat–Green Party coalition to power in 1998). Nevertheless, over time, environmental issues have consistently increased in importance in polling in Germany, even when they temporarily slip back from the top rankings due to problems such as joblessness.

In the United States, environmental regulations run the danger of being seen more as a part of the problem than of the solution, more a piece of the Washington bureaucratic establishment than a forward-looking philosophy of green job creation (explaining, for example, the rise of free-market environmentalism). The Environmental Protection Agency (EPA) grew from its founding in 1970 under President Nixon from a staff of about 8,000 and budget of $455 million in 1972 to a staff in 1995 of 18,000 and an operating budget of $4.5 billion—the seventh largest in staff and third largest in budget in the federal regulatory system.

Furthermore, founded as a pollution control agency, the EPA has no power to oversee comprehensive environmental planning, but has programs that are called 'media-specific' aiming at water, air, solid wastes, toxics, etc. The existing regulations favor 'end-of-pipe clean-ups' such as filters or waste-water treatments installed later, rather than preventive pollution measures, which would grow from social ethics and be more likely to stimulate the creation of cleaner production processes and technologies (Schellman 1995).

Under the Clinton administration, the standards for cleaning up major 'Superfund' pollution sites have been so strictly interpreted that water must be restored to drinking-level purity even if it never was at that level of purity to start with, motivating industries to set up plants on virgin land without the legal risks of the formerly hazardous Superfund sites. The stick is paramount here, not the carrot. And if the 'crime' is a huge one, as in the case of General Electric (GE)'s pollution of the Hudson River with PCBs (making the fish uneatable and killing birds that eat the fish), the company is even tempted to argue, as did GE, that the billion-dollar fine and clean-up are too large and burdensome for any one company to handle, and are, therefore, 'unfair'. Meanwhile, GE is responsible for some 83 Superfund sites throughout the US that need to be cleaned up. The social order is characterized by classical, *laissez-faire* antagonism between business and government on environmental issues rather than by mutual incentives for long-term cooperation. The best that can be said for this is probably incorporated in the revolutionary 1973 Clean Water Act designed to protect all US waterways: this law gives any citizen the right to bring any company to court for pollution for a fine of $25,000 per day if the firm is found guilty. But how many citizens know of this right or are motivated by social ethics to file a suit? *Laissez-faire*—leave it alone—is what they are most 'pre-programmed' by their culture to do.

While properly constructed regulations can encourage innovation through re-engineering, as business professor Michael Porter has argued, this appears to be the exception more than the rule in an open free-market society where regulations are only haphazardly enforced (Porter 1991). Indeed, the free-market environmentalist school of thought can be interpreted as an American reaction against governmental environmental regulations that have been misapplied and threaten to get in the way of entrepreneurial flexibility.

Germany was stimulated by the discovery of the collapse of the forest ecosystem in 1985 to create the world's most stringent environmental regulations. Some 50% of the nation's forests were dead or damaged by air pollution and, like Japan, Germany has a 'forest culture' which shapes utopian blueprints or visions of the ideal society. Green movements proliferated, symbolized in part by the Green Party, which was successful enough to enter the *Bundestag* in the 1994 elections and is now the minority coalition partner in the government of Gerhard Schröder. Chancellor Helmut Kohl pushed environmental regulations ever since his initial election in 1982, despite his party's conservatism, stimulating the movement for environmental regulations. He created the Federal Ministry of the Environment, Nature Conservation and Nuclear Safety in 1986, supported, in turn, by the Federal Environment Agency, the Federal Research Center for Nature Conservation and Landscape Ecology, and the Federal Office for Radiological Protection. All the extensive environmental regulations have to pass both houses in the federal parliament, the *Bundestag* and the *Bundesrat*.

Clearly, the German public is more interested in environmental regulations than is the American public (Mueller 1995). The German regulations attempt to integrate the concepts of economic growth and environmental protection in cost-effective ways. Some regulations involve economic incentives (such as positive tax treatment of unleaded gasoline). Other regulations are voluntary agreements (such as the deposit refund system in the beverage industry). And, sometimes, the voluntary measures become mandatory (such as the Packaging Ordinance of 1991 which makes it compulsory for producers to take back or recycle packaging). The German system appears closed enough to the entrepreneur that environmental reforms work as both carrots and sticks. For the assumption is that, within Germany, the environmental laws are systematic, will be enforced and will be too difficult to get around to be worth trying. The social market economy has fostered a *de facto* green growth economy in comparison with most other national economies in the world.

German regulations appear to be better oriented for stimulating the creation of environmental businesses and green jobs than the American system of environmental regulation, partly because the environmental ethic has been more internalized in the German population and is easier to enforce given greater social solidarity and consensus than is the case in the United States. By integrating their environmental regulations with economic realities, the Germans have succeeded more than any other population and are positioned to become world leaders in environmental business, exporting some 40% of their environmental technology business (OECD 1992). Germany has already established a leading position in exporting environmental technology (Mueller 1995: 36; *The Economist*, 20 November 1993: 81). This leadership is symbolized by Germany's 1.6% of GDP spent on environmental investment—more than any other large industrial country.

As a nation based on ideas, a tradition stemming from the Enlightenment, Americans may first have to be motivated by an ideal of environmental utopia and social ethics in order to achieve a social consensus of environmentalism and political regulatory system that is less reactive, less splintered, less after-the-fact, and more proactive, preventive and comprehensive. Free-market environmentalism may be a necessary starting point in order to motivate green growth in socially oriented start-ups such as The Body Shop in Britain and Ben and Jerry's in the United States (see Chapter 1, §C2). These social entrepreneurs from the Anglo-American individualist, free market tradition try to set social examples, perhaps to make up for the absence of such social policies on the part of the nation-states in which they are based.

F. Sometimes Small is Beautiful

The ultimate example of social entrepreneurship is, perhaps, the Scott Bader Commonwealth in the UK. This story is described in the chapter on alternative forms of ownership at the end of German economist E.F. Schumacher's classic in environmental economics, *Small is Beautiful*. Schumacher wrote: 'We always need both freedom and order. We need the freedom of lots and lots of small, autonomous units, and at the same time, the orderliness of large-scale, possibly global, unity and co-ordination' (Schumacher 1973: 53-54). Drawing from Eastern as well as Western thought, Schumacher was critical of the Western humanist tradition (epitomized by Luc Ferry): modern Westernization forces people to experience themselves not as a part of nature but as outside forces destined to dominate and conquer it. Technological and scientific illusions of progress have caused human beings to confuse income with capital: they live off irreplaceable capital they find in nature and which they do not produce (such as fossil fuels).

Schumacher's strategy was to break up the large macro-economic abstractions, such as the Gross National Product, into small work and entrepreneurial units which put people first, with technology limited to what is appropriate for the local situation. The classic example he used, the Scott Bader Commonwealth, is a cooperative enterprise of deliberately limited size that actually constitutes a small commonwealth based on social and political as well as economic and technical tasks:

1. The *economic* task: to bring in orders that can be designed, made and serviced in a way that results in profit.

2. The *technical* task: to provide marketing with a constant flow of up-to-date designs which permits them to continue to bring in orders.

3. The *social* task: to give members of the company opportunities to participate and develop in the working community.

4. The *political* task: to inspire other people to change society by providing them with an example of economic health and social responsibility.

Thirty-one years after founding Scott Bader in 1920 as a producer of polyester resins, alkyds, polymers and plasticizers, Ernest Bader decided to make radical changes. He wanted to overcome capitalism's abstract power to reduce all people into the managed versus the managers and to get around the invidious notion of a 'labor market'. So he turned the 161 people who worked for him overnight into 'partners' or, more precisely, members of a Scott Bader Commonwealth which he established with a constitution declaring that:

a The firm would remain of a size limited enough so that every person could embrace it in mind and imagination—about 350 people.

b The salary ratio between lowest and highest paid could not vary beyond a ratio of 1:7 before taxes.

c No member of the commonwealth could be dismissed except for gross personal misconduct; but anyone could leave voluntarily giving due notice.

d The board of directors of the company would be fully accountable to the commonwealth, which confirms or withdraws appointment of directors and agrees to their level of remuneration.

e No more than 40% of net profits from the firm would be appropriated by the commonwealth (leaving 60% for taxation and self-finance within the company) and one-half of these profits would provide bonuses for those working within the company and the other half given to charitable purposes outside the Scott Bader Organization.

f   None of the products of the company could be sold to customers known to use them for war-related purposes.

For the twenty years following these changes, the company continued to prosper (and continues to do so today) with the normal ups and downs, seeing the staff grow to 379, and setting up several small new firms. The aim of Scott Bader was not massive profit, but to create successful businesses with social responsibility which put people first and avoided the reductionism of the private ownership system.

I personally discussed the virtues of the small-is-beautiful ideology with economist Simon Whitney of New York University in the late 1970s just before he died. Whitney forecast that big business mergers would soon overwhelm the small-is-beautiful model. His projection proved to be accurate. At the end of the twentieth century, merger mania has spread throughout the industrialized world. Mergers cannot really be said to be 'beautiful'. And, as the merger trend peaks and the inevitable post-speculative reaction sets in, E.F. Schumacher's model of small, meaningful work-sites that husband the resources of particular places on the earth by limiting technology to what is really needed and doing 'economics as if people mattered' is apt to re-emerge as a useful strategy for cultural integrity and personal ethical satisfaction.

Thus, private utopias such as Thoreau's 'Walden' have evolved and become industrialized from rustic log cabins to becoming mini corporatist city-states. In the cases of The Body Shop and Ben and Jerry's, as they move to their second generation of ownership, legal and media problems plague their managements as their entrepreneurial efforts develop from the creative to the maintenance stage and size itself becomes a problem with their emerging multinational status.

What is necessary in order to motivate the founding of environmental businesses in a free-market environment is, however, by no means sufficient for social responsibility in the majority of cases of corporate development in liberal democratic societies, as Mancur Olson's thesis of individual and small-group self-interest suggests. Of the total number of businesses, those that can be classified in the 'win–win' category in which both business and the environment benefit are in the minority and may appear more prominently in certain historical phases of economic development than others.

G. Win–Win: Factors Four to Ten

We live in a world in which the 20% of the population in industrialized countries use 80% of the world's resources. Therefore, it is the particular obligation of these rich resource-users to find 'win–win' solutions to the conflicting claims of business profit and environmental responsibility. Win–win strategies minimize resource use, maximize green objectives and simultaneously increase profits and competitiveness.

Ernst Ulrich von Weizsäcker, Amory Lovins and L. Hunter Lovins argued in their 1997 report to the Club of Rome, *Factor Four*, that it is possible to double the global standard of living while cutting resource use in half through practical, imaginative measures that would use resources at least four times as efficiently as is done at present. They give fifty detailed examples of quadrupling resource productivity ranging from hypercars to hot-climate houses to super-refrigerators to lower-energy beef, fans, pumps, motor systems, to strawberry yoghurt, biointensive minifarming, electronic mail and durable office furniture.

The hypercar concept aimed to improve the 80% of the fuel lost before it gets to the wheels: in 100 days, fifty experts from General Motors in 1991 built two four-passenger cars with ultra-strong, ultralight composite materials with twice the normal efficiency, excellent safety and cleanliness, comfort, style and sporty performance. The Clinton Administration's Partnership for a New Generation of Vehicles provided support for the big three US automakers to develop a car with tripled efficiency within ten years (although the individual car companies are expected to do even better than this privately).

Often, we forget the basics of productivity—the key to building economic wealth. In any business system, we can double productivity either by cutting the inputs in half while producing the same amount of outputs; or we can double the amount of output with the same quantity of inputs. *Factor Four* proposes, in effect, using not half the inputs but merely a quarter, causing a huge spurt in productivity and wealth through resource efficiency. Counter to the trend of the big mergers, which create high stock value by doubling the size of the firm and then reducing the number of workers by half, von Weizsäcker, Lovins and Lovins suggest:

> We need a rational economic incentive that allows us to employ more people and fewer resources. Businesses should sack the unproductive kilowatt-hours, tonnes and litres rather than their workforce. This would happen much faster if we taxed labour less and resource use correspondingly more (1997: xxiv).

Not all scientists are convinced that reducing resource use by a factor of four is sufficient for long-term sustainability. Some suggest a factor of ten. The German Friedrich Schmidt-Bleek concludes that material turnovers should be reduced by 50% on a global basis. Given that further increases in world population are inevitable and that per capita consumption is some five times higher in OECD countries than in developing countries, he maintains that sustainable levels of material flows cannot be achieved unless the material intensity of OECD countries is dropped by a factor of ten. He therefore founded an international 'Factor Ten Club' in Carnoules, France, in 1994, advocating a factor ten reduction target for material sustainability based on an efficiency revolution through eliminating subsidies on resource use and a new perception of welfare.

Three non-profit organizations in Germany—MISEREOR, BUND and the Wuppertal Institute—published a 'Factor Ten' book in 1996, *Zukunftsfähiges Deutschland* ('A Germany Fit for the

Future', BUND/MISEREOR 1996), in which systematic means and measurements are presented for lowering resource use by 80%–90% by 2050. In their view, the eco-crisis is not just technical or managerial, but is a crisis of the inner world, of values and how we interact with each other. The faster, greater possibilities of travel lead us to set more distant goals: we are always travelling faster on the way to spending ever shorter periods of time, leading to constant stress. As a consequence, the desire to save time puts pressure on the environment. Gene technology is used to speed up the growth of tomatoes. Frozen fast foods involve heavy energy use in freezers. Other kinds of cost efficiencies involve environmental sacrifices: crabs taken from the North Sea, for example, are transported first to Morocco where the labor to take them apart is cheaper before being reimported into Norway to be sold as fresh North Sea crabs (consider the transportation burdens on the environment). More than 3,500 kilometers of transportation can be involved in the production of just one pint of strawberry yoghurt. This factor ten consortium advocates using tax reform to shift entrepreneurial incentives towards more eco-responsible, energy-saving products. They propose regional use and regional specialization to reduce transport costs from exotic imports. The motto changes from 'Think globally; act locally' to 'Consume regionally; sustain the globe'.

H. Eco-Development Phases

In *Environmental Strategies for Industry*, Kurt Fischer and Johan Schot identify two American eras of environmental management. (1) The first is the phase of 'resistant adaptation' from 1970 to 1985, when companies merely complied with new environmental regulations of high technical specificity, often showing resistance; (2) the second is the phase of 'embracing environmental issues without innovating' extended from the mid to late 1980s, when companies were able to make easy but significant improvements—setting up the promise of 'win–win' solutions (Fischer and Schot 1993).

For example, from 1989 to 1991, Texaco was able to reduce its combined air, water and solid-waste streams by 40% and its toxic emissions by 58% through pollution-control equipment, better control systems and an improved waste-reduction process. But, as Walley and Whitehead have argued, and McKinsey and Company surveys confirm, the third phase of environmental management throughout the 1990s is more likely to be characterized as one in which environmental compliance and improvements became much more expensive and, therefore, it takes more than the optimistic ideology of win–win to get managers willingly to sacrifice profits for heavy green costs (Walley and Whitehead 1994a, 1994b; McKinsey & Co. 1991). Thus Texaco planned to invest $7 billion up to 2000 on environmental compliance and emissions reductions—three times the book value of the company and twice its asset base.

The global trend towards free market privatization, competitiveness and economic growth regardless of social consequences may just reinforce Olson's principle of rational selfishness, threatening to push win–win environmental solutions off the map of the perceptions of the upwardly mobile. The Asian economic crisis beginning in 1997 with the fall of the Thai currency and collapse of its banking credibility and the spillover to Malaysia, South Korea and Indonesia increased perceptions of global economic uncertainty. The explosion of nuclear bombs in tests in India and Pakistan the following year heightened the uncertainty and pushed perceptions away from economics to national security concerns for the first time since the Gulf War: the win–win strategy risked being overwhelmed with the lose–lose dynamic of another nuclear arms race.

But, even if win–win options are in the minority from a realistic business viewpoint, they must be held up as an ideal goal. And, since perceptions are relative to time, place and historical circumstance, we must try to pin down a logical, universal ethical stance on which we can agree no matter what our stage happens to be in the eco-development cycle and no matter in what kind of business or economic activity we happen to end up.

Before suggesting such a set of ideal logical ethical propositions (see Chapter 4), however, it may be best to consider what has been done to date to evolve such an environmental standard through consensual, voluntary mechanisms. One means of arriving at such a standard is the establishment of environmental management auditing systems designed to move companies towards green logic in order to achieve certification by an international authority. The following chapter examines the advantages and disadvantages of perhaps the most developed of these auditing processes: the European Union's Environmental Management and Audit Scheme (EMAS).

Chapter 3
The Limits of EMAS
From the Risk-Reducing Environmental Certification of German Enterprises to Risk-Provoking, System-Transforming Ecopreneurship[4]

This chapter is based on interviews conducted with German companies that qualified for the EU's Eco-Management and Audit Scheme (EMAS) by 1997. Six key theses summarize our evaluation of EMAS followed by conclusions and recommendations.

■ *Thesis 1.* EMAS contains both intended and unplanned side-effects which stimulate innovations and symbolic corporate values. Therefore, it does more than merely increase the efficiency of the existing system.

---

4. This chapter is co-written with Alexander Keck and was originally published in German in *UmweltWirtschaftsForum*, September 1997, by Springer Verlag. Victoria Hottenrott ably assisted in the translation. The companies included: GETRAG Getriebe- und Zahnradfabrik (an automobile distributor), APU GmbH (a refrigerator recycler), Boehringer Mannheim GmbH (a pharmaceutical company), ADtranz (a Daimler-Benz transportation company), ABB Kraftwerksleittechnik GmbH (an electricity transmission technology company), Heidelberger Schloßquell-Brauerei GmbH (a brewery), ABB Gebäudetechnik (technical equipment for buildings), Blanco GmbH (sinks made out of compounds), Rudolf Wild Werke (a fruit juice company), and SCA Hygiene Paper GmbH (a hygiene paper company, the only firm for which no *oral* interview was granted).

- ☑ *Thesis 2.* EMAS—in its function as an appropriate quality label for certain companies—is an improvement over other existing systems.

- ☑ *Thesis 3.* EMAS serves primarily as an instrument to minimize risk and cost in conservative, risk-averse German society with the main goal of reducing insecurities.

- ☑ *Thesis 4.* EMAS is pursued vigorously in times of financial health and is dropped quickly from the agenda once the company's situation becomes more problematic.

- ☑ *Thesis 5.* EMAS is nothing but an extension of the ISO series: a process is added, which reduces vulnerability by distracting criticism of a lack of corporate social responsibility.

- ☑ *Thesis 6.* EMAS will fall into obsolescence if its credibility and relative legitimacy as a 'green label' are not strengthened.

A. Introduction

Once upon a time there was an Environmental Management System by the name of the Eco-Management and Audit Scheme (EMAS). Those were the days of brand names, quality seals and pseudo-environmental standards such as ISO 14000. To validate or not to validate was the predominant question. The process of validation was generally perceived as a mechanism for reducing company risk short term and for maximizing ecological (eco-) marketing possibilities. This amounted simply to the pursuit of reformism: continuous striving for improvement within existing systems. Validation represented a systematic distraction away from those entrepreneurial strategies that would have been needed the most: the radical challenge of high entrepreneurial risks in the short run, in order to minimize environmental risks according to the criteria of sustainability in the long run.

However, for German entrepreneurs, the decision whether or not to aim for an EMAS validation of their companies took place merely in the context of the regular management process and was a extension of the ISO 9000 series, which was mainly concerned with achieving more quality, savings in materials, and innovative efficiency improvements within the closed compass of existing production systems.

At best, German entrepreneurs using EMAS as an instrument aspired to be trendsetters, not revolutionaries or system transformers. And, while this attitude may be understandable in an era of great financial uncertainties and global competition, the inability of the EMAS resolution to provide elements beyond the scope of the existing frame is a potential contributory factor to its own self-destruction.

B. Methodology

In the spring of 1997 we conducted an intensive qualitative study interviewing the ten German firms in the Rhein–Neckar region that had been certified under EMAS by the end of 1996. Our goal was to uncover the motives behind the decision of managers to strive for a validation of the company, and to analyze the resulting costs, benefits and consequences. These questions were of particular significance at the time, given the 1998 revision of the EMAS guidelines by the European Union.

The interrogation of German firms was significant, since about 75% of all firms certified in Europe are located in Germany. Instead of a quantitative analysis embracing all 300 certified German firms, our strategic approach consisted of a qualitative study of all firms certified by 1997 in one region. This approach served to exclude variations due to regional differences. Secondly, a spontaneous impression as to what role EMAS can play in management practice and nurturing environmental orientation was made possible. Other studies have shown that most of the companies involved with EMAS have concentrated their efforts on the technical reduction of material use and emissions through so-called 'end-of-pipe' technologies. Measures within a production-integrated environmental protection (PIUS)[5] approach more likely represent an exception. Professor Jürgen Freimann of the University of Kassel, Germany, concludes: 'Managerial measures introducing a process of continuous improvement have not yet reached a level of importance necessary to carry out the paradigm switch to preventive environmental care' (Freimann 1996).

The underlying EMAS logic asserts that, for more and more voluntarily participating companies, the rising intensity of the application of environmental management systems finally results in a transformation process. The assumption is that growing quantity finally produces qualitative changes, which ultimately represent a paradigm shift. However, one is tempted to ask if and how such a paradigm shift can take place without a catalyst or a model that actually illustrates a living example of the successful changes. One of our central assumptions is that specifying the ideal standards or models serves to enhance the impulse for transformation.

C. 'Ecopreneurship'

Before all else, a distinction has to be made between 'green businesses'—established businesses, which become increasingly environmental only after their initial founding—and *green–green businesses*—businesses whose conception, from the very beginning, is an environmentally friendly one, and who strive for a social and ethical transformation of that particular business sector. Green–green businesses are founded by 'ecopreneurs', who themselves become catalysts for the transition from the mere continuous improvement of the old existing production process

5. PIUS is an acronym from the German term *Produktionsintegrierter Umweltschutz*.

through constant technological efficiency gains to pioneering eco-economic solutions that are suitable as paradigms or exemplary solutions for a social transformation. Green–green businesses and ecopreneurs can therefore best be understood as 'ideal types' in the sense of sociologist Max Weber or as standards, which will hardly ever be found as 'pure' types, but rather 'typify' or characterize those businesses that fall into these specific categories. As ideal types, green–green businesses and ecopreneurs can serve as a fixed point or maintenance base of collective learning, that is to say as value clusters, which are capable of steering the continuous *process of legitimization of the perception and will of a society*.

Such standards can, for example, be helpful in changing managerial attitudes in the business culture away from the risk-reducing maximization of quality toward a risk-provoking vision of socially and ecologically responsible economic prosperity. Ecopreneurs and green–green businesses turn away from merely fortuitous collective learning, which is steered on a basis of individual rationality by speculative and free-rider motives and seeks the greatest material profit or the lowest costs, regardless of social and ecological consequences.

Examples that come close to a green–green business include The Body Shop and Ben and Jerry's in the Anglo-American world, and Spinnrad, Waschbär and Neumarkter Lammsbräu in Germany. The category 'ecopreneur' is well illustrated by Anita Roddick, the founder of The Body Shop, and Ben Cohen, associate founder of Ben and Jerry's. Both ecopreneurs are social activists, who aspire to restructure the corporate culture and social relations of their business sectors through proactive, ecologically oriented business strategies. As a consequence, individuals not formerly participating in the market become involved and markets are created for products that are eco-sensitive with respect to resource use, process design and distribution. Ecopreneurs pursue social and ecological goals by means of profit-oriented businesses. This business strategy involves the ecopreneur 24 hours a day, and implies a mode of living that is wholly dedicated to the socially symbolic business. The ecopreneur has determined that, given that setting up any business for oneself requires absolute devotion in the first few years, this time might as well be simultaneously directed towards social and ecological goals, rather than just towards income production.

Businesses with such a green–green focus will attract the media's attention and will benefit from a free-rider use of this publicity, since their competitive advantage lies in having embodied an ecological orientation in their core business objective. Therefore, this ecological orientation cannot be compromised, for it is functionally essential and detached from prevailing external circumstances. By definition, green–green businesses have to be innovative. Flowing from environmental consciousness, they have to realize inventions that either relate to their components or systemically expand or newly define the concept of quality in ecological terms. Negative externalities will either be eliminated entirely or, compared to conventional businesses, reduced significantly at all stages of the production–consumption cycle. The governing perspective is rather to achieve positive externalities, which will make the business clearly identifiable as 'green–green' among all its competitors (see Pastakia 1996: 4).

Triggered by the ecopreneurs, the enthusiasm of employers and consumers alike pushes questions concerning financing into the background. The central concern becomes the 'ability of society to sustain the original enthusiasm and efforts of individuals and institutions, which eventually determines whether or not it is willing to make the transitions to more sustainable patterns of economic activity' (Pastakia 1996: 4)

This ideal image of the ecopreneur was used in the quantitative interrogation of the selected businesses as a basis in order to detect how close the motives of these eco-audited firms are to those of an ecopreneur, and to assess the nature and intensity of any obstacles. The questionnaire was developed with the help of Dr Dieter Roth, director of Forschungsinstitut Wahlen and editor of the *ZDF Politbarometer*. It consisted of a quantitative as well as a qualitative component, focusing, however, on the quantifiable and measurable. Nevertheless, due to the change of paradigms embodied in the definition of the 'ecopreneur', one has to anticipate that qualitative questions are more useful in providing hints regarding approaches and obstacles to the possible *process* of a system transformation than are the quantification of the motives that are derived from the 'actual state' or hindrances stemming from this 'actual state' to a more developed ecological orientation. The nature of a change in paradigms as a flowing transition process and the divergence of the status quo from the ideal originally posited cannot be measured by an established means of measuring intensity if a sufficient theory of the adaptation process between the two fictitious fixed points, the real and the ideal image, is not yet extant.

The quantitative results were based on 'closed' types of question and turned out to be insufficient, considering our aspirations of identifying the circumstances for a paradigm shift and of relating them to the status quo. In contrast, open-ended qualitative questions enabled us to gain insights that go beyond the conventional antiquated point of view, giving some notion of what an approximation to the ideal could look like in the future—what the ideal circumstances might be for potential ecopreneurs. These insights permit us to come to some judgement as to what EMAS can possibly contribute to the ideal picture of the ecopreneur, and where, on the other hand, the limits are of the framework assumed by EMAS.

D. The Progress and Deficiencies of EMAS

We cannot claim to present identifiable progress or deficiencies completely, nor can we make a definite statement about their relative importance on a higher quantitative level. However, the certified businesses of the Rhein–Neckar–Odenwald *Kreis*—despite their limited number—may give us important clues about what businesses can currently achieve in developing a more environmental orientation with the help of EMAS, and what kind of obstacles may arise that may hinder progress or encompassing involvement.

Thesis 1

EMAS contains both intended and unplanned side-effects which stimulate innovations and symbolic corporate values. Therefore, it does more than merely increase the efficiency of the existing system.

Innovations can be a clear sign of a transition from mere talk to environmental production. But the implications of innovation can by themselves raise management concerns about uncertainty. Promoting innovative research means constantly questioning and analyzing the new terrain and, if necessary, deserting it. EMAS supplies businesses with an effective tool, creating a framework for action that truly promotes environmental innovation. A central step within the EMAS process, which is being stressed by firms as an unconditional requirement for the generation and implementation of environmental goals, is the 'implantation' of environmental consciousness in the minds of all staff (Ritzenfeld 1997). It is important to establish a sense of responsibility on the spot, which is essential in guiding the permanent innovative potential of employees directly involved in the production process.

To be able to extract a definitive plan for realizable ecological improvement from various suggestions, the eco-audit and the internally authorized representative both serve as triggers and as points of crystallization of diffuse environmental knowledge within the organization. The environmental manager's exploration of this knowledge is legitimized through EMAS, and the informants at all levels derive motivation from a new, institutionalized corporate value, shared by all: corporate environmental consciousness. By becoming a planning parameter, the environmental orientation subtly informs the overall conceptual planning process, as is the case at Boehringer Mannheim. Here, variations in the products are discussed by the conceptual planning team, and so the internal representative for environmental concerns can influence the thrust at an early stage. EMAS therefore guarantees the necessary institutionalization of ecological goals in the planning process, preventing the emergence of problems at a later stage that require costly changes.

The inherent challenge of EMAS constantly to develop and design new environmental goals finally suggests 'interpreting continuous improvement as a duty' (Müller 1997), thus activating potential within the business to generate improvement especially in those situations 'when technical and financial resources' (Müller 1997) are exploited. For example, the *inventive* potential to develop the new locomotive ECO 2000 already existed at ADtranz even before EMAS was considered; however, it was not until the inherent dynamics of EMAS were introduced that the actual *innovation* was stimulated. This innovation had higher chances of success due to the environmental management system established simultaneously.

Consequently, at the GETRAG company, their own Innovations GmbH was created, focusing mainly on the weight reduction of gear units and higher efficiency. Conceptually, the design combines advancing entrepreneurship in the market with dynamic environmental goals. In this case, of course, one is advocating the shift of the business away from measures that merely fulfill the legally required technical standards ('state of the art') towards the best available technology with respect to environmental suitability.

Thesis 2

EMAS—in its function as an appropriate quality label for certain companies—is an improvement over other existing systems.

Ecological quality becomes a significant factor in decision-making about different versions of a product, or different versions of production processes—if, ultimately, the most ecological alternative is selected. EMAS places this understanding of quality in a more operational context: stimulating the emergence of environmentally positive reactions that have to be communicated to business partners and integrated into forward (distributor) and backward (supplier) relations. These external effects inherent in EMAS can explain the surge of cost-intensive adaptation processes, which, moreover, cannot be passed on to the consumer: Boehringer Mannheim abolished products containing mercury, even though the actual concentration was far lower than the level at which companies are required to declare it on their labels. Hence, industrial clients would not have to have the slightest concern regarding possible contamination of sewage water treated with Boehringer pharmaceutical products.

EMAS symbolizes a kind of environmentalism that becomes part of the customer's demands in such a way that certain forms of exploitation of the environment are perceived to be incompatible with the new eco-image. By the same token, however, EMAS constitutes a framework for developing and presenting measures to respond to very specific, ecologically motivated requirements of customers. The company ADtranz finds itself confronted with calls for material analysis, for exclusion of certain substances and concepts for taking back waste which—within EMAS—not only must be carefully planned and effectively presented to clients, but furthermore are subject to a take-back and recycling programme with a 30-year time-span.

EMAS serves as an indicator of relative ecological quality, and contributes to a calculation of price that goes beyond mere raw material cost. And a more competitive strategic position is obtained once the declaration of environmental goals becomes part of contracting. At the same time, any partial progress documented within the EMAS process is marketable and produces immediate marketing gains. It is remarkable that such environmental advancements are implemented regardless of the expected actions or reactions of competitors simply to avoid any loss of credibility during the highly sensitive process of conversion to an ecological strategy.

The image enhancement aspect, however, has made it obvious that EMAS functions almost exclusively as an ecological extension of the ISO quality management series. It therefore plays an important role in inter-business relations, however negligible this may be with respect to the final consumer, who will 'always expect products of high quality and does not care to be involved any further' (Eisenbach 1997). Evaluations of suppliers therefore become the result of the strategically required definition of 'where we are heading in our development'

(Ritzenfeld 1997). If the goal is to build up an understanding of quality that includes an additional ecological component, then this process is facilitated by automatic acceptance as a supplier based on an EMAS or ISO 14001 certification. In this way, additional supplier evaluation through questionnaires or actual site visits can be eliminated or reduced to a minimum. The key again lies in establishing a trusting relationship with the aid of the public communicative character of EMAS, as well as the opportunity to influence the environmental goals of the suppliers by passing on to them the requirements demanded by end customers.

Whereas previously, when purchasing highly dangerous MMA (methylacrylat), the Blanco GmbH company had to ensure, on-site at its supplier's premises, that waste was not disposed of in an inappropriate manner, it has now found a validated British supplier that could be accepted immediately and maintained automatically as an 'A Partner' (i.e. unrestricted trade partner). As regards acquiring quality standards, the importance of EMAS increases the greater the toxicity or danger of a substance or process. Hence, it 'might challenge the eminent position of the ISO 9000' (Müller 1997).

Thesis 3

EMAS serves primarily as an instrument to minimize risk and cost in conservative, risk-averse German society with the main goal of reducing insecurities.

Monitoring the flow of resources, evaluating potential environmental risks and obeying ever-changing environmental legislation is necessary in order to determine all preventable environment-related costs and risks and to ensure the preconditions for ecologically oriented management of the business. However, this requires a systematic framework that provides an extensive flow of information. EMAS is a useful instrument for illuminating the structure and conditions of production.

Since information and knowledge acquired by environmental managers through EMAS happened to be estimated in times marked by recession, one can presume that the pursuit of environmental goals has a cost-reducing potential, stemming from a restriction of resource use without lowering production output.

As well as directly reducing the use of raw materials, EMAS provides information for creative integration of environmental data into the materials handling process: Before EMAS, the GETRAG company, for example, had an insufficiently aggregated set of data and registration of costs. EMAS became the catalyst that initiated an entire restructuring of production processes from wet- to dry- process technology, along with a reduction of emissions and waste-water to almost zero. EMAS therefore functions as a stimulus to think of new ways of increasing efficiency within the business as well as at client level. In both cases, resources are conserved and the competitive position is thus improved. Environmental targets—as laid out in the audit and the recorded data—and the continuous search for technical advantages are mutually supportive.

The crucial factor—determining the extent of cost reduction—probably depends on how high disposal costs are: for example, at ADtranz, ceasing to use halogen-containing cables and switching to biodegradable 'Esteroele' created a competitive advantage, especially with respect to its clients. However, for Boehringer, the recycling of polluting solvents—technically possible within the firm—was not economical because of the costs involved. Pharmaceutical companies such as Boehringer, where industrial environmentalism has a long tradition, seem to prove that, even in highly committed businesses, the reduction of waste to reduce the cost of recycling or the enhancement of income sources from meticulously separated fractions will eventually face limits. Indeed, many pharmaceutical companies have already exhausted all available potential. Recycling beyond that point may either be impossible because of legal or technical limitations, or involve higher costs than the purchase of new material and the incineration of waste.

Moreover, the market mechanism itself can restrict even these win–win opportunities—the simultaneous improvement of environmental protection and business profits—in various ways. Take the case of the 'Caprisonne' brand of fruit juice. With respect to EMAS, reducing to a minimum the thickness of the aluminum layer in the packaging remains the environmental goal, which, due to failed attempts to recycle aluminum, represents the most environmental and at the same time most economic solution.

EMAS is almost inevitably linked to the collection of data, which has hitherto not been carried out on a regular basis. This new depth of analysis, performed routinely, allows for immediate detection of irregularities and contributes directly to preventive environmentalism. EMAS not only systematically facilitates the tracking of individual or partial processes, but simultaneously requires a holistic assessment of the company.

This assessment should preferably be conducted with the help of environmental indicators that are clearly attributable to specific sectors (e.g. Caprisonne). However, the variation of the indicators among different companies leaves room for data cosmetics: if there are certain numbers or certain data per sales-unit in which the environmentally conscious client is more interested, a presentation per revenue-unit that merely considers internal savings can effectively cover other things up.

The high ranking given to legal security within the company is documented by Ritzenfeldt's categorization of production inputs into raw materials, purchased parts, energy/air/water, and external legislation. But the unconditional demand by factory management for high legal security has also been confirmed by other firms. And, although everybody agrees that the German legal framework contains too many details, these very regulations are the crucial factors that guarantee the desired legal safety. Many believe the main purpose of EMAS is that it simplifies the maintenance of existing regulations perceived to be relevant in the environmental area. On the other hand, there is disappointment that, despite certified high diligence in complying with environmental laws stemming from EMAS, the competitive advantages hoped for have not materialized, not even with respect to orders placed by local governments.

EMAS has helped most firms realize that many laws, even those that are clear and unambiguous, have not been taken into account, due to the huge quantity of such regulations. But this fact had not even been picked up by the state authorities responsible, who, in addition, were not able to provide information on specifically what rules and measures were relevant to a particular firm. Managers disapproved of the expression 'with respect to the economic environmental aspects', frequently used in environmental regulations, which leaves too much room to fall short of 'state-of-the-art' measures. Such vagueness could demotivate and irritate those businesses that strive towards complete assessment and strict observance of legislation.

Thesis 4

EMAS is pursued vigorously in times of financial health and is dropped quickly from the agenda once the company's situation becomes more problematic.

One manager (Franz Seifermann of APU GmbH) spelled out the ups and downs of the economic in relation to the political environment with which the environmental consciousness inherent in EMAS regulation is confronted. A few years ago in the 'green capital', Freiburg, old refrigerators were delivered to the APU company because of its extremely environmentally friendly disposal process—as certified by EMAS. Now, however, price differentials as low as 20 pfennigs (around 10 cents) per refrigerator provide enough justification to use other firms instead, even those with clearly inferior procedures. A strange component of this phenomenon is that, in times of financial distress, the idea of ecological validation is not even followed consistently by its own creator (the state), as becomes obvious with public procurement: a community in the Rhein–Neckar *Dreieck* dispensed with transporting old refrigerators all the way to Hamburg to a disposal company with lower prices but clearly ecologically inferior technology, but only because of the higher cost when transportation was taken into account.

On the other hand, in facing globalization, the private sector cannot be expected to go any further than making the environmental focus that is manifested in EMAS a decisive factor if two offers have the same price. However, it is unlikely that increasing globalization will lead to a higher willingness to pay. A consideration of a company's environmental strategy will be particularly unlikely in those cases where an industry relying on export sells to regions with little or no environmental awareness. By the same token, the environmentally oriented company itself has to use global sourcing to remain competitive (Isaak 1993: 17ff.). This is especially important if the client has the market power to signal a very specific willingness to pay, resulting in a larger profit margin, depending on how cheap the input components have been.

With respect to competitiveness, EMAS cannot enforce regional procurement, even though it might well be more ecologically desirable, as long as, for example, the ingredients for juice concentrate of equivalent quality can be imported by the Wild Werke more cheaply from China or from the Philippines, even after taking into account all shipping costs. The international price competition today forces businesses such as the Blanco GmbH to divest of their traditional Swabian suppliers and substitute European competitors—facilitated by the increasing integration of the EU. Also, the home competitive battle is increasingly being fought on international markets, and therefore against foreign competitors, which are still using the cheaper inputs: those inputs that ABB, for example, would have scruples against using due to their environmental unfriendliness.

What remains is the preliminary exclusion of these problems from the environmental goals of EMAS and instructions that are biased towards 'supply management, to focus on prices' (Brümmer 1997) to prevent competitive disadvantage and decay. A continuous and permanent environmentally oriented strategy, however, is hardly going to be achieved by such priorities.

The significance of environmental protection within the management of a business today has been reduced to an insurance scheme for the firm due to the maximization of net present value (NPV). This affects most negatively those medium-sized businesses that try to improve their position through eco-audited innovative strategies. In particular, the larger banks, when consulted about finance projects, are demanding an increasing amount of security and guarantees from smaller businesses, in contrast to large corporations (which is part of the trend to maximize NPV). An eco-audit of a small business, based on ambitious, innovative environmental goals, appears, relatively speaking, to be more risky and prompts risk-minimizing, NPV-maximizing banks to undertake periodic revisions of the credit conditions. Even if installment payments are made on a regular basis, they may go as far as to threaten to call in the loan, which will put the small entrepreneur under pressure. In comparison, an integration into larger corporations through acquisition is much preferred and recommended. In addition, this opens up the possibility of subsidizing the acquired small business, supporting price dumping against an independent, more innovative competitor.

Thus EMAS is not only incapable of taking on the role of a credible competitive parameter, which could make a continuous environmental focus economically worthwhile: in what is initially an increasingly positive competitive arena for environmental credentials, EMAS is also likely to be diluted down to a minimal compliance with minimum requirements and therefore lose its value step by step. EMAS is the luxury child of good economic times and may soon be treated as an orphan.

Thesis 5

EMAS is nothing but an extension of the ISO series: a process is added, which reduces vulnerability by distracting criticism of a lack of corporate social responsibility.

A truly legitimate interest in EMAS as a marketing tool or instrument of Total Quality Management does not necessarily have to go beyond that definition. Even without a genuine interest in a comprehensive and continuous shift towards environmentalism, the desired results can be achieved.

If one looks, for example, at the attitude of the management of the Heidelberger Schloßquell Brauerei GmbH, it becomes clear that it was the striving for the certificate, specifically the label, rather than for the implemented measures themselves that was important, as long as the validation helped to push the firm towards a predominant position among beverage producers. The central unit of the company rejected an offer by the Baden-Württemberg Department of Agriculture to provide financial and marketing assistance based on the requirement that—as an environmental goal—the firm would commit itself to purchase raw materials exclusively from organic sources in the region. The positive effect on image was evaluated by the management as marginal compared to the risk of committing only to regional suppliers and of losing the flexibility of 'global sourcing'.

Similarly, there does not have to be a contradiction between the eco-image, cultivated through the acquisition of EMAS, and the dismantling of the malt-making facilities of the Heidelberger Schloßquell-Brauerei. These facilities originally had optimal conditions for production: the farmers of the region cultivated special rye in exactly the amount needed for which they had long-standing supplier contracts. If one looks at this traditional, environmentally friendly structure of production from the company's perspective, however, the malt-making facilities were inevitably seen as overcapacity due to alternative global sourcing possibilities available.

Therefore, market logic suggests the pursuit of measures that are easiest to implement within the market situation as well as the least risky, interfering as little as possible with conventional market behavior, as long as this is sufficient for obtaining the locally based certificate and, beyond that, achieving the spillover effects of an environmentally oriented company. Environmental protection in this context is understood as an extension of quality, but 'within the limits of financial possibilities' (Neckermann 1997), not as proactive behavior independent of the situation. Nevertheless, there still remains the possibility of obtaining public recognition for an environmental focus through the measures certified and monitored by EMAS.

Thesis 6

EMAS will fall into obsolescence if its credibility and relative legit-imacy as a 'green label' are not strengthened.

While ecological superiority (as a counter-strategy) is the most striking feature that distinguishes an ecopreneur clearly from his or her industry, and which at the same time accounts for more attention paid by the media—a factor that can contribute greatly to the business's development—EMAS does not provide for anything comparable, which would make a company stand out in any systematic way from its competitors. The political context and the auditing concept seem to relate in such an unsatisfactory way that one should not expect too many impulses for the creation of a meaningful instrument to emerge from this quarter.

EMAS is legitimately associated with the environmental focus of a company: a focus, however, that, in the first instance, consists only of the creation of formal systems such as the designation of an environmental manager, the establishment of an incentive structure for innovation, and open communication channels for suggestions. At Heidelberger Schloßquell, for example, expanding the quality manager's responsibilities into environmental fields—within each division—by formally assigning him the second title of 'environmental manager' was one of the first steps of the auditing process. The aim was to provide for clearly assigned responsibilities to protect against legal problems. However, most of the responsible staff at this point hardly had any idea of the meaning of their new mandate. It is therefore reasonable to suspect that, because of administrative overload associated with EMAS (complaints such as 'we can only react' [Neckermann 1997]), resources and capacities were no longer available for truly proactive modernization. Consequently, changes in product design were rare: bureaucratic formalities surrounding the implementation of more or less symbolic processes 'would already overwhelm the individual employee' (Brümmer 1997).

It might make more sense to conceive of a higher evaluation unit which would visit the businesses and monitor the evaluations of the environmental expert, and which might even request testimonies from suppliers. Even if it is administratively possible to perform only random checks, the threat of effective comparability would stir up the industry immensely (Müller 1997). This could constitute the first step towards an industry-specific referential benchmark of an environmental thrust, which could give an insight into what would be possible with respect to environmental protection within that particular industry. Such a system would also make proactive strategies far more attractive for the individual company. The need for this change stems from the fact that the EMAS does not provide for a gradual approach with respect to different ecological measures, except for creating the comparability mentioned earlier through enhancing publicity. But gradual approaches are often the only effective means of achieving results in this area. The Blanco GmbH, although not subject to a take-back obligation, nevertheless, as part of its customer service policy, collects old plastic sinks when new ones are purchased, and these can be recycled and put back onto the market. Still, it would be absurd to expect customers to prefer a recycled sink to a new one, since the color is not consistent (it has a mottled appearance) and the price may even be higher. As in the case of sprays and the problems with FCC (fluorchlorcarbonate), a benchmark must first be established as to what could be a more transparent ecological solution for the handling of plastics.

In a country saturated with products, as Germany is, where there is a natural demand for excellence in terms of both price and quality, the ecological solution will only succeed if its environmental superiority is effectively communicated, if it is clearly distinguishable from others, and if, because of this, its attractiveness increases. EMAS, however, is not capable of documenting these ecological factors, and even less capable of serving as a basis for comparative exceptional treatment under the law, such as deregulation. Yet an integration of EMAS into an eco-political concept implies exactly such meaningful interconnections. Politically, 'certain things have to be laid down: mere coaching and the principle of voluntarism are not the right way to go since in the long run voluntarism will wear out' (Brümmer 1997).

There must therefore be a vision of a probationary phase of instigating an environmental focus for which EMAS is used, which ultimately promises to lead to deregulatory or other product-promoting effects. Instead, today we have a 'heap of disconnected laws which conjures up the impression that a law will evolve only when everybody is ready for it' (Götz 1997). Young and dynamic companies, however, state that they would appreciate it 'if concepts that were considered to make sense would consequently be enforced, even if not everybody could follow suit' (Götz 1997).

With this complete lack of integration of EMAS into an overall eco-political concept, there should not be any surprise over why it cannot assume the role of a deregulator. By the same token, there is little encouragement for any business to believe that it might actually realize economic benefits—that is, see its green business strategy pay off appropriately compared to its competition.

E. EMAS is a process legitimizing the system; ecopreneurship is a transformation of the system.

A central focus of EMAS lies in cost/risk-reduction through a higher level of transparency and more efficient modes of production. This has the side-effect of reducing the harmful impact that an enterprise has on the environment. Implicitly, this thrust assumes 'a pervasiveness of inefficiencies' in the enterprise 'which we do not at all find convincing' (Oates *et al.* 1995: 120). A similar conclusion is reached in a detailed empirical study by McKinsey (1991). Fischer and Schot (1993) typify such developments as the third phase of entrepreneurial pollution control: the encouragement to aim for win–win opportunities leads to the dangerous misconception that there are unlimited possibilities of improvement on the operational level, which have merely been unnoticed thus far, and will pay off previous efforts in a fairly short period of time. On the other hand, Fischer and Schot point out the importance of a radical long-term restructuring of businesses with a continuous focus on an environmental strategy for effective environmentalism. This requires taking into account large investments along with long periods of amortization, since the easily achievable successes of the initial efforts have already been largely exhausted since they were first put into action in the 1980s.

While EMAS—with very basic requirements—sets the entry barriers at a low level, at the same time it implicitly suggests a successive fine-tuning of previous modes of production *à la* win–win strategy, especially if thus far only very few ecological modifications have been undertaken. EMAS can be seen as the unimaginative extension of the conservative, risk-reducing certification process of ISO. The ecopreneur, on the other hand, detaches him- or herself deliberately from the conventional system of the production of goods of a particular industry in order to be on the front lines of a counter-strategy of system transformation, which hopes to be able to draw its financial success from that very confrontation. The progressive component of auditing as the trigger of acquiring and crystallizing knowledge, of employee motivation, improvement of planning, and organizational perfection of innovative potentials will not be exploited to convert the counter-culture of the ecopreneur into a positive model of proactive pursuit of breakthrough ideas and technologies. That is, the appeal of EMAS stems exactly from the insecurity within that flexibility: the insecurity of whether or not one could actually be a free-rider on perceptional incompetence with minimal effort, which is nothing more than building up 'seeming more than being'—an absolutely rational form of behavior.

The concentration on vanishing win–win opportunities and diminishing ambitions (inevitably linked to this process), as well as the use of EMAS for mere image purposes, makes the validation a transitional fad, since the concept of continuous improvement does not affect long-term restructuring, but is understood and practised as a long process of postponement of structural adaptation. The process of changing the normal ambiguity in environmental matters by restructuring through EMAS should not be seen as completely negative, since a continuous improvement can mean at least an impulse towards an environmental reorientation within longer time-frames.

This restructuring process is particularly relevant to larger businesses, whose bureaucratic and technological inflexibility tends to inhibit the 'creative destruction' of a market economy, according to Schumpeter (1950). However, small dynamic businesses certainly face the risk that EMAS works too well, meaning that it satisfies the psychological needs of those involved for an environmentally oriented focus that seeks approval or reduces the uncertainty about ethical obligations. By making it possible to have 'normal industrial processes certified as ecological' (Hallay and Pfriem 1993: 51), the system transformation—which is more likely to be initiated by small businesses, is deferred. For nobody is making the case for the ecopreneur, certainly not the people distracted by EMAS.

The consequent preoccupation with 'refining a museum' distracts from the possibility of restructuring so that those dynamic entrepreneurs are mobilized, who—as ecopreneurs—are willing to assume the responsibility of serving as role models.[6] A good example is represented by the manager at APU GmbH, Franz Seifermann, whose original motivation stems from his personal realization that relevant production can be designed in a much more environmentally sustainable way. Or, in the sense of Schumpeter, neither profit motives nor financial aspects were originally the crucial stimuli, but rather the mere desire to acquire power. Such are the various motives, within the institutionalized concept of eco-auditing, that reward or even demand

---

6. Being a role model could, for example, mean to become—through one's economic activity—an essential part of a *Faktor Vier* ('factor four') concept in the sense of Weizsäcker (Weizsäcker *et al.* 1997).

those 'breakthrough' technologies to steer the continuous process of collective learning towards more environmentally friendly schemes. Technological leaps, however, which pave the road for a change of the innovation paradigm, are not encouraged within this existing EMAS framework, which does not have any gradual incentives and therefore does not make essential changes of the product attractive (see Hemmelskamp *et al.* 1994: 210ff.). EMAS should therefore focus particularly on start-ups, who still operate at the beginning point of the creation of a value (-adding) chain and thus are much more likely and able to integrate their environmental design pragmatically than are older established companies. Established firms already have their place in a value chain and may therefore not be flexible enough to achieve massive environmental reorientation since they lack the necessary influence to pass these new policies on effectively within the vertical supplier structure.

EMAS itself is an appropriate instrument for industrial reorientation in a society such as Germany's, which is used to 'real' institutions, whose specific requirements have to be met, and seems to appreciate them as an effective stimulant (Isaak 1997a: 11). The present preoccupation with what *could* happen may predestine a society, fostering such cultural schemata, for the creation of a 'green market', incorporating an extensive definition of quality, risk reduction and other attributes of a prevention of ecological dangers—even generating a demand for environmental controls. However, the shift to an 'unraveling of such a green market' itself faces a lot more cumbersomeness than in a society 'where counter-culture is part of culture like in Great Britain or the US' (Isaak 1997a: 5ff.). Within the context of globalization, due to the need for competitiveness, EMAS furthermore runs the risk of being overwhelmed by a *laissez-faire* liberalism without a 'social vision of community of some sort . . . to guide one's freedom and natural free-rider instincts . . . Instead one's energies are quickly diffused and even one's economic victories are socially meaningless' (Isaak 1997a: 12). EMAS seems almost to have reached this point, rather than bringing about a convergence of the environmental consensus already inherent in German society, a consensus with respect to social responsibility and latent entrepreneurial energies, including positive 'free-riding' within the context of system transformation.

As currently designed, in the form of a final program directed towards obtaining the certificate while minimizing result-oriented efforts (see Hemmelskamp *et al.* 1994: 207), EMAS punishes and hinders the evolution of ecopreneurial potential with competitive disadvantages—particularly the lack of political support through the creation of a consistent framework. Academia tends to make more out of EMAS than it is, increasing the number of participants and becoming part of the problem, instead of being the midwife for the solution. It does this by holding back evidence of miscalculations in the way EMAS operates: interpretational flexibility is designed in such a way that it paves the way for a development contrary to the resolution's original intentions (see Hemmelskamp *et al.* 1994: 224).

F. Results and Recommendations

The progress and the deficits on the way to a greater corporate concentration on the environment cannot be viewed in isolation from influential groups, which confront the corporation and influence the meaning and the role of EMAS. Therefore, it is crucial to think in terms of socio-cultural changes when aiming at ecologically satisfying corrections of the means of production. A problem-solving potential, which would stimulate latent ecopreneurs with external incentives to exert their role as 'change agents', can be found in the make-up of the societal system: in the market, and in the demands articulated within it, in the social ethics, and in the state.

Since it is not realistic to expect a permanent presence of 'green–green' businesses in the market due to the lack of competitiveness, it is advisable to establish political assistance, if society as a whole can be assumed to support the existence of these kinds of entrepreneur. A deregulation of business-related rules should only take place where there is proof of an environmental orientation, meaning the existence of obvious comparative advantages with respect to environmental friendliness. This is why the accessibility of venture capital for start-ups should be supported in order to give clear signals in favor of creativity which already faces high risks and to counter the distortions of competition in imperfect markets. Financial start-up incentives linked to ecopreneurship as a requirement for eligibility can be interpreted as the usual necessary free-rider behavior of a start-up entrepreneur taking advantage of public subsidies, but differentiated by remuneration based on positive external effects on society. Competitiveness will still depend on the delivery of highest quality and lowest prices; hence the environmental effort can only be a supplementary one. Big corporations, on the other hand, can be forced through such public subsidies to establish a green–green business sub-unit, which is not part of the 'normal' business logic and which includes the generation of positive external social and environmental effects.

All of these proposals have in common the idea of furthering creative 'freewheeling', as was the case at IBM with its establishment of the Entry Systems Division ('Come back with a PC!') as a 'special operating unit—an independent "company within a company", free of close IBM control' (Kotler and Armstrong 1991: 537), except that it should have an environmental bias. 'It developed a culture and operating style similar to those of its smaller competitors . . . ignored [IBM] traditions and did many "non-IBM-like" things' (Kotler and Armstrong 1991: 537).

These measures will be the easier to implement, the more public ethics as part of social capital are receptive to an environmental orientation. 'Social capital makes communities more effective' (Putnam 1995: 124). For the goals of cultivating an environmental orientation and its entrepreneurial implementation, a strengthening of social capital 'will be more effective than a comparable increase in spending' (Putnam 1995: 124). 'It is too much to expect that masses of young people will swarm into ecopreneurial careers without social support and highlighted role models' (Isaak 1997a: 13), which could happen, for example, through a presidential award scheme, and through the introduction of 'ethical economic training at schools', which could create an environment in which 'green–green businesses . . . are perceived as viable, legitimate solutions to career choice uncertainty and global unemployment' (Isaak 1997a: 13).

However, to reach their full value, the present recommendations require, above all, the realization that, because of the disappearance of win–win opportunities, structural change is inevitable, and does not even have to be sidelined, as is often asserted, for so-called economic reasons—provided that the state takes on the exclusively external role of a reliable preventive environmentalist. Contrary to conservative approaches, companies do not simply obtain from the government technical knowledge about existing modes of functioning, but environmentally related knowledge for a better orientation; if it happens in any other way, the state acts as an interventionist and suppresses entrepreneurial activities.

Crucial for operationalizing these above proposals is an upgraded EMAS procedure and certificate, which indicates the degree of environmental orientation and makes it administratively more transparent. Various bureaucratic resources will then have to be reorganized with respect to their responsibilities in such a way that they can track down relatively ecological businesses on the basis of their documentation within the validation process, a process that to date remains in the domain of pressure groups (see Steger and Winter 1996: 43). EMAS has the task of making intrinsic environmental motivation 'not acknowledged [otherwise] transparent; otherwise, such environmentally oriented persons . . . feel . . . ridiculed and their activity rejected inducing them to reduce it' (Frey 1992: 169). It is critical to prevent latent ecopreneurs from refraining from sending their signals challenging current business practice and from failing to appear as effective 'change agents', just because they are suppressed—on behalf of a misleading one-dimensional perspective of competition stemming from 'creative destruction'.

Chapter 4
Ethics

Tractatus Logico-Ecologicus[7]

1	The world is everything that has been sustained.
1.1	What has been sustained has resulted from a collection of low entropy and export of high entropy or disintegration.
1.2	The collection of low entropy can result from syntropy or an integration of energy targeted towards economic development that is 'sustainable'.
1.3	Unsustainable development destroys the world through uncontrolled, undifferentiated entropy.
1.4	Unsustainable development results from actions that do not take long-term systemic consequences into account.
2	Ethical human action is action that results in sustainable development which takes long-term systemic

---

7. Inspired by Ludwig Wittgenstein's *Tractatus Logico-Philosophicus* (1922). As with Wittgenstein, there is no claim here that anything is 'new' and no sources are cited since the author is indifferent as to whether or not others have had the same thoughts before him, given the objective: the purpose is to reduce the number of these thoughts as far as possible while yet retaining the logic of the whole, indicated by the numbering of the parts.

consequences into account, countering undifferenti- ated entropy in the world by focusing on the outcome after at least two generations.

2.1 Undifferentiated entropy in the world is manifested in uncontrolled flows and accumulations of things that are potentially destructive.

2.12 Social ethics is the critical task of learning how to use things or technologies constructively, rather than destructively, or of learning not to use them at all.

2.13 Ethics refers to individual action that is characterized by goodness and justice.

2.131 Social ethics refers to the collective traditions of good- ness and justice that characterize a community.

2.2 Countering uncontrolled flows and accumulations of destructive things requires institutional regulation and enforcement of social ethics that transcends the self- determination or freedom of individuals.

Just as the freedom of individuals is limited by social ethics enforced at the community level, and the auton- omy of communities is limited by social ethics regu- lated at the nation-state level, the sovereignty of states in a global political economy is limited by an inter- national code of social ethics.

3 Human beings are rationally motivated to be free- riders within communities and to participate in shar- ing collective goods while paying as little as possible.

3.1 Anarchy is an area ungoverned by generally accepted codes of social ethics in which individuals set their own laws and free-ride at will on the world's resources.

3.12 The free-rider, unrestrained by global institutional laws or enforceable regulations, is free to act in ways that result in undifferentiated entropy articulated in the accumulation and exchange of destructive things.

3.121   But the free-rider can also be an entrepreneur who creates syntropy that leads to economic growth and prosperity. Such syntropy is usually an unintended by-product of individual, profit-maximizing behavior.

3.2   The free-rider must be given incentives to act ethically outside the realm of enforceable international laws in ways that do not result in the accumulation or exchange of destructive things and which do result in economic growth and prosperity leading to development sustainable for at least two generations.

Entrepreneurship can be transformed into a moral act that sustains the earth and the people who live upon it.

4   Moral entrepreneurship can only grow to a critical mass if economic and political incentives clearly support the ethical free-rider and deter the free-rider tempted by the greater short-term rewards available for accumulating and exchanging destructive things.

4.1   The increasing spread of literacy and technology throughout the world's population, and the status of working for lower wages as supply increasingly exceeds demand on the labor markets, reduces the amount of difference in wages necessary as an incentive to stimulate the free-rider to be ethical and the entrepreneur to be moral in terms of sustaining the earth.

4.2   As the amount earned for being ethical approaches equality with the amount earned for free-riding on the earth in a short-term fashion, social and political incentives can tilt the balance to stimulate ethical, that is, sustainable entrepreneurship.

4.3   Social and political incentives for sustainability require the identification of criteria that promote development providing universalizable standards of sustainable opportunity for at least two generations and systematic effort to promote perceptions and schemata of collective learning that support such development.

4.4   Collective learning is the social process of differentiating legitimate patterns of adaptive behavior in order to manage environmental change without losing cultural integrity.

4.41   Cultural integrity is made up of traditional patterns or schemata.

4.411 Schemata are prototypes of meaning or value clusters that process information and brand it with particular interpretations.

4.2   Social ethics involves transforming cultural schemata into contagious commandments characterized by sustainable principles of good and just behavior.

One universal principle presupposed by such commandments is that individuals should act in such a way that their behavior can be read as a general law for all human beings, particularly serving the interests of their grandchildren and the world they will inhabit.

5   The world will become everything that has been sustained in the eyes of our grandchildren.

Chapter 5
What is to be done?

To recall where we began: a human being can only stand in one place at once. Ideally, one should take a stand on an 'Archimedean point' of leverage that maximizes life-chances for oneself, one's family and one's community. A green perspective provides such a point of leverage—a set of strong values that takes us beyond the objective of mere democratic contentment or materialistic upward mobility. Green logic can become a taken-for-granted, natural assumption for all that one undertakes. For our starting position, from which all else follows and which helps to give life its meaning, should also constitute a set of universal guidelines for individual and collective behavior. In order to be responsible to one's children and grandchildren—to sustain the earth—one has little choice but to start out with a green position.

But the globalization of the world economy, characterized by privatization and corporate mergers, often appears overwhelming to those who would assume a green stance. Globalization has decreased the leverage of governments in effecting environmental issues, shifting power to big businesses. And the big businesses most aware of environmental issues are those who are likely to lose the most if the market goes green (that is, companies supplying virgin raw materials or goods and services that most intensively tap resources or the environment). Moreover, even under the best scenario in which the biggest, most influential companies lead the way to make the markets greener, we run into the dilemma summed up by Australian Philip Sutton of Green Innovations Inc.: that there is no such thing as an ecologically sustainable company—only an ecologically sustainable society. Sustainability is a phenomenon that involves a whole system (Sutton 1997).

So we must begin at the beginning with the simplest of principles that will enable us to socialize society as well as firms and governments in order to make their markets sustainable. To be effective, these principles must be few in number and integrate green ethics with green economic growth, short-term action with long-term development.

Building green from scratch is the basic starting point. This is what schoolchildren must be brought up to desire to do. This is what governments must subsidize. And this must become the basic means for long-term sustainable competitiveness and competitive advantage for the business community. Ecopreneurship starts at home, in the house, in the car, in the school, at work, in the local and regional economy. The ecopreneur is a symbolic, even existential, change agent who gives meaning and direction to social interactions. From the old maxim 'You can't go home again', the ecopreneur learns to accept a new maxim for the twenty-first century: *'Everywhere is home.'* Each of us must be brought up to have a stakeholder sense of responsibility for the earth which gives us sustenance in order to sustain it to give our grandchildren sustenance.

Yet the problem is that, today, many have no place they can call 'home', so who will do the socializing to make them view the whole earth as home? People are so mobile for the sake of freedom or job opportunities or professional advancement that they leave home after home behind. They become accustomized to placelessness, where everything seems to be available everywhere. The paradox is that, to create a sustainable environmental humanism for the future, the assumption of rootless universality, which originated in the French Revolution and which dominates the West and Westernization, must be modified to nurture loyalty to green roots locally and regionally. We must go from homelessness or placelessness to an arbitrary place we call 'home' in order to understand why it is vital to see the earth as home. Just as it is asking too much for an individual to assume responsibility for all future generations and just as it is, therefore, appropriate to stress the concrete world of one's own grandchildren, so it is demanding too much for a human being to identify with the whole earth as home before he or she knows what commitment to his or her own home (or homes) is all about. We can free-ride on the earth without ever investing in any permanent responsibilities. But this does little good for one's children or children's children. We become, literally, 'spaced out'.

Buy green. As consumers, we should select products that harm the environment least. Avoid purchasing a sports utility vehicle or light truck which pumps 60% more CO_2 into the atmosphere than the average car. Ask for paper bags rather than plastic at the supermarket. The plastic bag may well survive longer than we will. As a producer, one should use environmentally certified suppliers wherever possible. We should walk or bike rather than drive whenever we can. We must transform economic and lifestyle choices into visible votes for a sustainable future. Creating green demand develops green markets.

Green logic inevitably confronts other conventional logics which it must seek to transform. The logics of fast growth, high consumption and instant gratification all undermine the long-term requirements for sustainability. Globalization overwhelms our perceptions to the point that we overreact instinctively through the maze of options like Pavlov's over-stimulated rats. There is usually little grace (which takes time) in this virtual adaptation, although virtual organization has become the very definition of competitiveness: producing customized results immediately for any anonymous customer. If speed kills the soul, we are in danger of creating a materially satiated, spiritless world.

Green logic slows us down to find a Zen moment of repose before each new endeavor is launched. This reduction of tempo permits genius to have time to develop and to come out first individually, then collectively. We must have time to let our best selves shine forth and to think through the energy, material and transportation requirements of our products and services in order to make them more resource efficient and eco-friendly. Green design flows from time for environmental development. Such designs involve creative, existential risks aimed at what some environmentalists call 'dematerialization': decoupling economic growth from further use of resources and reducing the amount of physical resources to the minimum to satisfy human needs. An example is the increasing spread and cost-effectiveness of wind-power machines plugged into electric utility systems which usually benefit from tax credits. Creative risk-taking in such green technology design begins from an arbitrary moment, an arbitrary place and an arbitrary cultural and organizational starting point—a stable 'maintenance base'.

In *Managing World Economic Change* (Isaak 1995), I have argued that, to build wealth and competitiveness in the world economy, one must systematically increase efficiency and reduce costs at the maintenance or home base of the organization, in order to free up capital, time and energy for new entrepreneurial endeavours, risk-taking and market creation. Sustainability provides such a criterion for cost-reduction, innovation and increased quality at the maintenance base. The motive for risk-taking often involves a search for freedom and autonomy that takes sustainability as a basic assumption.

Free-rider behavior is inevitable in a market economy and is one of the motivators for entrepreneurial risk-taking: the free-rider must be steered towards green logic through social ethics and government intervention in the form of ecotaxes and subsidies for ecopreneurship. Without regulation and a will to enforce social ethics through sanctions and incentives, there is little to dissuade those who would prefer short-term wealth from going into the drug trade or dealing in weapons of mass destruction. So the case for government intervention *per se* is obvious. But there are many schools of interventionism.

Free-market environmentalism is an Anglo-American school of thought that begins with the proposition that the least government intervention is best in term of utilizing the efficiency of private markets for environmental management objectives and avoiding the red tape and perverse incentives that can be associated with a government 'control economy'. With its stress on private property and reducing the costs of government intervention to increase competitiveness and freedom, this school of thought plays well in the post-Cold War era of Anglo-American-led globalization and privatization. These ideas have been indirectly reinforced by the studies of Andrew Warner and Jeffrey Sachs at Harvard who have demonstrated that open, export-oriented national economies grow much more rapidly than those that try to go it alone by protecting their economies from imports through high trade barriers (Warner and Sachs 1995). But, in terms of green logic, it is somewhat helter-skelter in effect and puts freedom and property rights before long-term sustainability as objectives. 'Pollution permits', for example, might be part of a solution to make the world a bit greener than it would otherwise be, functioning as a kind of indirect tax for firms that need to buy the permits of other (cleaner) companies in order to keep going down the road of business as usual. But there is something watered down here, similar to a hypothetical trade in traffic tickets to avoid losing one's driver's license. The aim seems to be more to avoid costs than to create greener ways of doing business out of principle. The pragmatism of the solution undercuts the legitimacy of the principle that is at stake, perhaps stimulating more strategies of avoidance than of proactivism. Nevertheless, it should not be rejected out of hand if the only political alternative is maintaining a pro-pollution status quo. Indeed, in the US in the 1990s, according to Larry Selzer of the Conservation Fund, there was a slow replacement of the word 'adversary' with 'partner' as environmental activists realized they had lost a significant amount of power and industrialists became tired of being portrayed in the press as the big, malevolent polluters and sought to influence legislation to find cost-effective, workable solutions to environmental problems (see Caudron 1995).

Entrepreneurial innovation and job creation may be stimulated by the free-market environmentalism school of thought. 'Freedom first' is a seductive siren call which may, however, ultimately bring the same dangers of distraction as did those classic sirens that tempted Odysseus—if freedom comes without the restraints of responsibility. Sometimes the free-rider pays with his life if he does not have the self-discipline to put on his safety straps first. (Odysseus, you will recall, strapped himself to the mast to avoid the fatal temptation.)

Going up the ladder of intervention, at the other end is *social market economy environmentalism* after the German model. Here, social order precedes freedom, just as the maintenance base is prerequisite to entrepreneurial risk-taking. The whole is perceived to be more than the sum of its parts—a systems view that *could* correlate nicely with sustainability. The Green Dot and Dual System of recycling in Germany, for example, are effective to the extent that people assume that these regulations will be systematically enforced. A green market becomes an increasingly integrated part of the social capital of the country. But, as noted earlier, the Dual System threatens to come unravelled at the end of the twentieth century because of an increasing number of free-riders who do not pay, increasing the cost of the system for those who do. In addition, too many people in Germany cut down drastically on accumulating trash: there is not enough trash for all the official recycling centers built and the price goes up for recycling, punishing the very people whom one wanted to encourage to recycle in the first place (the case in Cologne, for example, where recycling costs have increased by as much as 30% a year).

The competitive pressures of globalization undermine the social market economy. The 'systemness' of sustainability in one nation that has been at the forefront in maintaining green markets cannot easily continue if neighboring nations across open borders all have less stringently enforced environmental incentives and sanctions. Nevertheless, the green logic implicit in Germany's social market economy is perceived by the overwhelming majority of the people as a clear social obligation, and the Germans rival the United States in leading in world exports of technologies for environmental protection.

In the US, where the free-market environmental ideology was born, the priority of environmental issues has slid from one of the top three concerns to the fifth position or lower in recent public opinion polls. Environmentalism is perceived by too many as a distraction from or as an obstacle to making money and achieving short-term competitiveness rather than as an opportunity to actually reduce costs and maintain a leadership position in green products, technologies and markets. And if this short-term opportunistic position continues to reign in the US, which has a 'limelight effect' in its influence abroad like no other country, it will only be that much more difficult to persuade countries less developed economically that they can become competitive in a green fashion. Of course, *it may actually be easier to start green in emerging economies where socioeconomic innovations can be targeted for green niches from the outset*—as in the case of Costa Rica's emphasis on biodiversity in the pharmaceutical business.

Research demonstrates, however, that environmental concerns rise in priority in nations where the per capita Gross Domestic Product has achieved a certain threshold of economic development. For example, Grossman and Kruger at Princeton University found that communities with per capita GNP above $5,000 annually up to $15,000 annually are increasingly concerned with lower environmental pollution (Grossman and Kruger 1991). It is at this take-off stage of environmental consciousness where the policies of international agencies and developed countries aiming to increase global environmental responsibility have the first best chance of success. This implies, however, an obligation on the part of rich nations to bring all nations up to the environmental take-off point. And, to work, such policies must be 'user-friendly' in terms of the desires of local cultures for autonomy and meaningful work: they must provide alternative means of earning a living or of satisfying basic needs which are ecologically sound and they must be policies that flow naturally from the indigenous culture, giving it new stimulus and hope for sustenance and survival. User-friendly policies come from creating stakeholder motivation in ecopreneurship and cannot appear as 'foreign' policies. They are policies that stem from radical transformations of collective learning, not only on the part of the indigenous local people but on the part of the so-called more developed people who would enlighten them.

The ideal outsider who would foster ecopreneurship in developing regions of countries, rich or poor, enters not with a finished blueprint for Western-style implementation, but with an open menu for cooperative planning, together with the local elite and people. He or she is a facilitator with a fistful of user-friendly, culturally specific recipes for increasing jobs and local economic autonomy, educational strategies for meaningful work, practical plans for hygienic water, food, air and healthcare systems. The ultimate eco-consultant is a Robin Hood delivering positive green growth transparency, aiming to reinforce existing community strengths and resources with a cooperative plan for collective learning, setting up the situation for breakthrough development. He or she, for example, might help set up a local bank or chain of interconnected banks in a typically under-banked developing region. The agenda must initially be totally open so that the local elite and people will become stakeholders in *their* plan for development, and *empowered* to carry it out. Only the end objective is made clear: self-sustaining economic growth based on local cultural tradition which will improve the environment locally and regionally.

Since 'economic growth' may be perceived to be a 'foreign abstraction', its concrete elements must be broken down into specific tasks and jobs growing out of comparative advantage and local social and political traditions. For example, poor developing countries cannot afford the waste involved in over-fer-

tilization by the use of pesticides. Nor can they afford inefficient houses that utilize polluting sources of energy. The Eco-
Robin Hood will stress what Vygotsky called the 'Zone of Prox-
imal Development'—the set of tasks a person cannot complete
unguided, but can complete when guided or prompted with
hints, questions or examples (see Wertsch 1985). He or she is
a facilitator and catalyst more than a teacher, a mentor more
a consultant, a velvet green hand in the background more than
a pushy promoter. The tone is that of the indirect spirit of what
the Japanese call *nemawashi*—preparing the soil carefully for
change or transplanting so that the same roots will find better
sustenance, positioning and protection: ideas are talked through
slowly by all those who will be affected by the changes and
have to carry them out; hence they are implemented smoothly,
without surprise or shock. Whether at home or abroad, in rich
countries or poor, the management objective should be the same:
to create positive transparencies for green growth learning and
sustainable entrepreneurship.

**The key economic principle of green logic is to limit all
government subsidies for the private sector to green start-
ups, the 'green–green' businesses of ecopreneurship, let-
ting the private markets take care of funding all other
forms of business.** Despite the reduction in the leverage of
government spending in the post-Cold War, globalized economy,
whatever spending the government does undertake for job creation and the private sector should be limited to establishing
green businesses or starting environmentally oriented subsidiaries in existing businesses. For there is no moral justification for spending the tax dollars of citizens to subsidize businesses that are not sustainable or environmentally responsible
from the perspective of the world one's grandchildren will
inherit.

To the very extent that the leverage of the government is
increasingly limited in the economy, it must concentrate its priorities in order to have any impact at all and to increase its legitimacy among its people. By focusing on job creation via sus-

tainable businesses, the government can target employment to match its long-term developmental interests and legitimize its cultural integrity. Moreover, if the government, for example, lets the situation develop into a condition of value-indifferent *laissez-faire*, the fires set to rainforests in countries such as Indonesia, Mexico and Brazil will spread the effects of deforestation and air pollution beyond their borders, ruining their own stock seed and tourist industry and becoming a plague on their neighbors. And this does not even take the probable damage in terms of global warming into account. A number of studies suggest that, to contain global warming, CO_2 industrial emissions, for example, must be reduced to zero in the next 60 years, followed by an 80-year effort thereafter attempting to pull CO_2 out of the atmosphere on a net basis (see Enting *et al.* 1994).

Government efforts to certify environmental management processes, such as the EU's Eco-Management and Audit Scheme (EMAS), function as marginal improvements over the status quo but also serve to distract companies from radical innovation to set up green–green businesses or to motivate ecopreneurship. Such environmental certification schemes must target cutting-edge ecopreneurship as the activity to be promoted, not merely defensive, risk-reducing environmental incrementalism.

As we have seen in the German case, companies are often motivated to achieve environmental certification merely as a cover to head off social criticism, lawsuits and bad publicity. Even this motivation must be turned around and used to encourage businesses to become dynamically proactive in ecopreneurship, setting standards, leading the way as role models, and creating new markets as a result. National and regional government contracts, for example, could be issued only to companies that put ecopreneurship at the top of the list in their corporate mission statement.

The environmental certification process often results in surprising innovations for companies whose managers suddenly look at the world differently. But, because of the incremental nature of such environmental improvements, there is not enough incentive radically to recast processes of manufacturing and service on a model of ecopreneurship or green–green business (starting up again green from scratch). Yet environmental technology institutes such as the Wuppertal Institute in Germany, the Rocky Mountain Institute in the US and the Zero Emission Research Initiative (ZERI) in Japan have demonstrated that large changes can bring more profits than mere marginal improvements. In pushing for ecopreneurial leadership and not just the 'risk insurance' of environmental certification, managers find their creativity constantly stimulated and can sleep well at night knowing that they are working for businesses in which they would be proud to have their grandchildren involved. The Scott Bader Commonwealth in the UK is perhaps the ultimate example where the business becomes a mini city-state with partners instead of managers and employees and where social responsibility and environmental ethics are a part of the 'constitution' and company mission objectives. Small is, indeed, sometimes beautiful, as E.F. Schumacher has shown, despite the speculative merger booms of the large in the globalized economy. Joint ownership arrangements with employees also can have the effect of deterring takeovers of the small by the large.

Starting up one's own business offers the unique incentive of having one's own way and being one's own boss. Since one is going for broke anyway, usually seven days a week, one might as well do it the right way and use a green design, gaining free publicity from 'the green edge'. The Body Shop and Ben and Jerry's are masters of this 'free-rider' marketing strategy. Ideally, one conceives of a business that is also a good cause. One should be so passionate about the idea for the product or service that it becomes a natural ideology, the means to all dreams, a road to one's own piece of utopia. If one is, so to speak, creating one's own world anyway, it may as well be a sustainable world that one is proud to advocate and to advertise, a cipher of the soul. And successful ecopreneurs should be highlighted as role models in schools and national award ceremonies in order to nurture creative sustainability and legitimize green leadership by example.

Win–win strategies that are good for the environment and simultaneously good for business profitability and competitiveness may apply to a minority of cases, but these are the niches towards which one should aim. To aim for win–win green business objectives is to uncover existing social capital and cultivate it to its full potential.

The 3M company's Pollution Prevention Pays (3P) program has saved the firm more that $750 million since it was started in 1975 as a direct outcome of reformulating products and processes, redesigning equipment and recycling. The organization had faith in the existing stocks of 'social capital'—the embedded community trust, norms and networks that facilitate collective learning and the accurate targeting of local entrepreneurship. Word of 3M's success, in turn, spread and stimulated collective learning on the part of other companies, which saw it as a model. Dow Chemical's Waste Reduction Always Pays (WRAP) is an example of this advancement of win–win social capital. And Procter and Gamble, a manufacturer of detergents and personal products, reduced disposable wastes by over 50% in the 1990s while increasing sales by 25%. While these companies in no way qualify for the Weberian ideal type of 'ecopreneurship', the environment would clearly be worse off if they had not had enough faith in green logic to take a chance on win–win strategies.

The World Bank, International Monetary Fund and other international institutions (such as the European Union) should not give bail-outs or loans to any country whose government does not use the criterion of green entrepreneurship as a standard for domestic government subsidy and intervention. Only by putting such an ecopreneurship/ green growth standard up front can the 'moral hazard' dilemma be countered and the 'conditionality' of the key financial institutions in the world begin to recover legitimacy following their recommendations.

For the financial crises at the end of the twentieth century have stripped not only the budget but the credibility of international institutions that serve as 'lenders of last resort', particularly the International Monetary Fund (IMF). And global deflation, which can easily spill into global recession and quickly into a depression, can only be countered with a confidence-building system of international credit, based on a stable currency. Even currency speculator George Soros, who became notorious for betting against the British pound to the point of making his view a negative self-fulfilling prophecy in 1993, came out in 1998 advocating support for and radical reform of the IMF and other world economic organisations in order to head off a looming systemic global economic crisis.

In the Great Depression, economist John Maynard Keynes wrote an essay entitled 'National Self-Sufficiency', writing 'let goods be homespun whenever it is reasonably and conveniently possible; and, above all, let finance be primarily national' (Keynes 1936: 758). However, soon thereafter he reversed himself arguing for a post-war system based on openness and convertible currencies. But his skepticism concerning financial flows remained and he believed that the budding IMF should restrict such flows in order to minimize the probabilities of international financial disturbances that could result in global, macro-economic instability. Globalization has realized his worst fears in the 'casino capitalism' that typifies financial flows in the world economy at the end of the twentieth century.

The need for restructuring international economic institutions was precipitated by an increase in demand for loans in times of financial and currency crises in the 1990s (by, for example, Mexico, Thailand, South Korea, Russia and Indonesia), an era of national budget austerity in OECD countries and an increasing predominance of the private sector as the main source of global finance. The crises are more numerous and costly, in short, than the amount of public funds available.

Yet this very need to be selective about which crises to fund and by how much creates an opportunity for influential policymaking for the sake of sustainability. Typically, the International Monetary Fund enters a country in financial crisis demanding an increase in interest rates, which presumably attracts foreign investors and lenders, re-establishing confidence in the economy, which, in turn, causes a currency that has fallen badly to rise in value. However, as economist Joseph Stiglitz of the World Bank has noted, the evidence that higher interest rates provide the right incentive for such confidence is less than overwhelming (*The Economist*, 11 April 1998: 52). And higher interest rates usually have the initial effect of requiring cuts in government spending and serve to slow down economic growth, putting thousands of people out of work who have a hard time understanding what their sacrifices are really for. Legitimacy, in short, is often lost. Massive political protests and instability frequently result. 'IMF orphans' are created—in South Korea, for example—where parents are dumping children they can no longer afford on the doorsteps of overwhelmed state institutions.

The concept of 'moral hazard' comes into play, since foreign investors anticipate that the International Monetary Fund will probably bail them out even if they make bad investments in volatile countries so they are less selective than they might otherwise be about which projects to invest in and not attentive enough as to whether the banks are well regulated and transparent in terms of up-to-date information. In the Mexican peso crisis in 1994, for example, the rich investors holding Mexican bonds were bailed out. By targeting green start-ups and eco-preneurship for special treatment, some of this loose, IMF-inspired investment can be shifted towards sustainability. And, in times of crisis, if the public must endure austerity measures, at least an argument can be made that sustainable private businesses are prioritized for support which will help the situation for their grandchildren, if not themselves. The IMF's virtue of currency 'conditionality' (or credibility) for stability's sake alone will not buy long-term domestic political support, whereas a socially responsible, green-job-creating focus will give any radical economic reforms required more legitimacy in the eyes of the public.

And the long-term legitimacy of international economic organizations is also critically important for the lending countries. How, for example, can the IMF deal with one American economist's suggestion that the US should not give any money to the IMF itself, which shuffles it onto government leaders and bureaucracies, but rather give $100 a month to every Russian citizen over 65 years of age directly? The IMF must become detached from being identified with rich elites in poor countries who are often corrupt and must make grass-roots follow-through in terms of sustainable job creation a prerequisite for lending. This would give it a proactive stance that would win votes rather than its current defensive reactive stance, which often appears to throw good money after bad, combined with a flourish of austerity measures that hit the middle class and the poor in the recipient countries the hardest.

As commentators throughout history, from philosopher Arthur Schopenhauer to economist Wilhelm Hankel, have noted, one cannot blame people who have no money for desiring it—particularly when they view it as a means to freedom. But what is less understandable is that wealthy countries that have money throw it at momentary crises as a panacea rather than regarding it as means to help satisfy *their own* longer-range needs— such as environmental sustainability. As Brazilian farmers and ranchers burned a record number of trees in the rainforests in 1998, government elites approached the IMF when Brazilian stock and currency markets were hit by the Asian/Russian contagion. It does not take a great deal of intelligence to assess which scarcity is the most significant: money can be replaced much more quickly than can tropical rainforests. Tropical rainforests have critical effects for the earth's environment for rich and poor countries alike. The IMF in such a case should not give a dollar untied to an ecopreneurial alternative to the destruction of the rainforests.

Advocating ecopreneurship is the same thing as building social capital. While government subsidies and tax incentives based on energy and materials use have much larger effects on the environment than do general subsidies to labor and capital, if job creation activities are explicitly linked to resource and energy-saving business objectives, a kind of 'win–win' political policy results: the more green job creation, the greater the subsidies. Such subsidies and tax incentives are particularly important, since only unique locations are able to pass the profitability test in sectors such as eco-tourism, genetic prospecting, and non-forest extraction. In Latin America, for instance, only when international externalities are taken into account, such as global warming, does sustainable forest management become profitable at the national level. The alternative is the status quo: forest clearings for agriculture with high long-run rates of return, even excluding government subsidies.

Government subsidies should be targeted to fund jobs in environmental research. Much more money is necessary, for example, to support studies to prove or disprove the endocrine disruptor hypothesis of Theo Colburn *et al.* (1997) in order to see to what extent certain chemicals in the environment have caused irreversible effects on human embryos. Empirical work is convincing in terms of alligators, mice, fish and birds. But what about human beings? Such research is what environmental humanism is all about. The unusually high number of women in the same location on Long Island in New York who contracted breast cancer stimulated the formation of a women's political movement among them. As a result, the US Congress funded an Environmental Protection Agency committee to come up with recommendations concerning Colburn *et al.*'s hypothesis and how harmful chemicals affect food and water. This signal, in turn, has many chemical companies concerned enough to push their own 'green' research agendas (whether the results are published or not is, of course, another matter).

Such environmental research may remain hypothetical for a number of years, as is the case with global warming. But, rather than risking potentially disastrous effects on the lives of our grandchildren, is it not better to do the research and to take precautions now if the evidence starts to mount and can soon be specified? Clearly, green logic is intimately connected with scientific developments, as well as with common sense. If chlorine, for example, were to be found to be responsible for a certain percentage of malformed human embryos, this would not necessarily be reason enough to ban chlorine, which is found in 40% of medical drugs sold in the US and effects some 45% of American businesses. But to create green businesses in order to find out which ways not to use chlorine for the sake of the health of humans and their environment would integrate scientific, economic and political wisdom.

As a species, we have presumably learned not to throw the baby out with the bath water when it comes to environmental regulation and protection. But, to keep our grandchildren smiling, it seems like the greater wisdom is to sin on the side of being overly cautious in terms of how we treat the environment and to tilt heavily towards funding ecopreneurs rather than to complacently accept the lottery of *laissez-faire*. If we do not aim for a green utopia, we are likely to end up with a brown dystopia by default. If we do not aim to create green jobs through the small and medium-sized businesses that create most new employment, we are likely to end up with jobs that undermine the earth's sustainability. And, if we do not set examples for our children as ecopreneurs, they will not have models of sustainability upon which to draw. We could do worse than to make our first principle *homo ecologicus.*

Bibliography

Anderson, T., and D. Leal (1991) *Free Market Environmentalism* (San Francisco: Pacific Research Institute).

Ashworth, W. (1995) *The Economy of Nature* (Boston, MA: Houghton Mifflin).

Berry, W. (1990) *What Are People For?* (New York: Farrar, Straus & Giroux).

Brümmer, P. (1997) Interview with P. Brümmer, Umweltschutzbeauftragter, ABB Gebäudetechnik AG, 25 March 1997.

BUND/MISEREOR (eds.) (1996) *Zukunftsfähiges Deutschland* (Basel: Birkhauser Verlag).

Cairncross, F. (1992) *Costing the Earth: The Challenge for Governments, the Opportunities for Business* (Cambridge, MA: Harvard Business School Press).

Camus, A. (1990) *The Myth of Sisyphus* (20th Century Classics; Harmondsworth: Penguin).

Caudron, S. (1995) 'The Green Handshake', *Industry Week* 244.17 (3 April 1995).

Cohen, B., and J. Greenfield (1997) *Ben and Jerry's Double-Dip: Lead with Your Values and Make Money, Too* (New York: Simon & Schuster).

Colburn, T., D. Dumanoski and J.P. Myers (1997) *Our Stolen Future* (New York: NAL-Dutton).

Davidow, W.H., and M.S. Malone (1992) *The Virtual Corporation* (New York: Harper–Collins).

Davis, J. (1994) *Greening Business: Managing for Sustainable Development* (Oxford: Basil Blackwell).

De Bono, E. (1990) *I am Right, You are Wrong* (London: Viking).

De Bono, E. (1994) *Water Logic* (London: Penguin).

Devall, B. (1980) 'The Deep Ecology Movement', *Natural Resources Journal* 20.2 (April 1980).

Egeln, J., *et al.* (1996) *Der Wirtschaftsstandort 'Rhein–Neckar Dreieck', Standortprofil und Unternehmensdynamik* (Schriftenreihe des ZEW [Zentrum für Europäische Wirtschaftsforschung Gmbh], 9; Baden-Baden: Nomos Verlag).

Eisenbach, D. (1997) Interview with D. Eisenbach, Stabsleitung Umwelt-schutz und Sicherheit, Boehringer Mannheim GmbH, 27 March 1997.

Enting, J., T. Wigley and M. Heimann (1994) 'Future Emissions and Con-centrations of Carbondioxide: Key Ocean/Atmosphere/Land Analyses' (Technical paper, 31; Melbourne: CSRIO Division of Atmosphere Research).

Faber, M., and J. Proops (1994) *Evolution, Time, Production and the Envi-ronment* (New York: Springer Verlag, 2nd edn).

Faber, M., H. Niemes and G. Stephan (1987) *Entropy, Environment and Resources* (London: Springer Verlag).

Faber, M., R. Manstetten and J. Proops (1995) 'On the Conceptual Foun-dations of Ecological Economics: A Teleological Approach', *Ecologi-cal Economics*, 1995: 41-54.

Ferry, L (1992) *The New Ecological Order* (Chicago: University of Chicago Press).

Fischer, K., and J. Schot (eds.) (1993) *Environmental Strategies for Indus-try: International Perspectives on Research Needs and Policy Implications* (Washington, DC: Island Press).

Freimann, J. (1996) 'Environmental Statements: Valid Instruments for Mea-suring the Environmental Management Success of a Company?' (Paper presented at the 5th International Conference of the Greening of Indus-try Network, Heidelberg, 25–27 November 1996).

Freud, S. (1961) *Civilization and its Discontents* (standard edn; trans. J. Strachey; New York: W.W. Norton).

Frey, B.S. (1992) 'Pricing Regulating and Intrinsic Motivation', *Kyklos* 45.

Fukayama, F. (1994) *Trust: The Social Virtues and the Creation of Prosper-ity* (New York: The Free Press).

German Advisory Council on Global Change (1995) *World in Transition: Ways towards Global Environmental Solutions* (Heidelberg: Springer Verlag).

Gersemann, O., and J. Ginsberg (1997) 'Ernst wie nie: Jugend 1997', *Wirtschaftswoche*, 15 May 1997: 1-2.

Götz, H. (1997) Interview with H. Götz, Werksleitung, Blanco GmbH & Co. KG 25 March 1997.

Grossman, G., and A. Kruger (1991) 'Environmental Impacts of a North American Free Trade Agreement' (NBER Working Paper, 3914; Prince-ton, NJ: Princeton University, Economics Department).

Habermas, J. (1971) *Toward a Rational Society* (Boston, MA: Beacon Press).

Habermas, J. (1996) *Die Einbeziehung des Anderen* (Frankfurt: Suhrkamp Verlag).

Hagel, J., and A.G. Armstrong (1997) 'Net Gain: Expanding Markets through Virtual Communities', *The McKinsey Quarterly* 1.

Hallay, H., and R. Pfriem (1993) 'Umwelt-Audits, Öko-controlling und externe Unternehmenskommunikation', *UmweltWirtschaftsForum* 1.3.

Hamermesh, D. (1993) *Labor Demand* (Princeton, NJ: Princeton University Press).

Hampden-Turner, C., and A. Trompenaars (1993) *The Seven Cultures of Capitalism* (New York: Doubleday).

Hemmelskamp, J., U. Neuser and J. Zehnle (1994) 'Audit gut, alles gut? Eine kritische Analyse der EG-Umwelt-Audit-Verordnung', *ZEW Wirtschaftsanalysen, Quartalshefte des Zentrums für Europäische Wirtschaftsforschung Mannheim*, Jahresverzeichnis 1994: 199-227.

Honey Bee 7.3 (July–September 1996).

Huntington, S. (1993) *The Third Wave: Democratization in the Late 20th Century* (Norman, OK: University of Oklahoma Press).

Huntington, S. (1996) *The Clash of Cultures* (Cambridge: MA: Harvard University Press).

Isaak, R.A. (1993) 'Virtual Organizations: From Entrepreneurial Networks to Strategic Alliances' (Paper presented at the International Symposium on 'Networking of Human Relations and Technology' at Tokyo Keizai University, 25–27 October 1993).

Isaak, R.A. (1994) *American Political Thinking* (Fort Worth, TX: Harcourt, Brace & Co.).

Isaak, R.A. (1995) *Managing World Economic Change: International Political Economy* (Englewood Cliffs, NJ: Prentice–Hall).

Isaak, R.A. (1996) 'Environmental Management from a Global Perspective' (Keynote address to the 89th AIESEC National German Conference on 'Environmentally Conscious Management', Bielefeld, 10 December 1996).

Isaak, R.A. (1997a) 'Entrepreneurship and Environmentalism: Germany's Social Market Economy vs America's Free-Market Liberalism' (Paper presented at 'Business and Environment' Conference, Southern Connecticut State University, New Haven, 15 November 1997).

Isaak, R.A. (1997b) 'Globalisation and Green Entrepreneurship', *Greener Management International* 18 (Summer 1997): 80-90.

Isaak, R.A. (1997c) 'Creativity and Entrepreneurship across Cultures: Logics of Perception, Green Growth and Utopia', in Dieter Wagner (ed.), *Bewältigung des Ökonomischen Wandels* (Munich: Rainer Hamp Verlag).

Isaak, R.A., and A. Keck (1997) 'Die Grenzen von EMAS', *Umwelt-WirtschaftsForum* 5.3 (September 1997): 76-85.

Kao, J. (1989) Entrepreneurship, Creativity and Organization (Englewood Cliffs, NJ: Prentice–Hall).

Keck, A. (1997) 'Fortschritte und Defizite auf Weg zu mehr Umweltorientierung von Unternehmen im Sinne des Ecopreneurship nach Isaak' (Unpublished thesis: Heidelberg: University of Heidelberg).

Knoke, W. (1996) *Bold New World: The Essential Road Map to the 21st Century* (New York: Kodansha International).

Kojéve, A. (1968) *Introduction to the Reading of Hegel* (trans. J.H. Nichols; ed. A. Bloom; Ithaca, NY: Cornell University Press).

Kotler, P., and G. Armstrong (1991) *Principles of Marketing* (Englewood Cliffs, NJ: Prentice–Hall, 5th edn).

Lager, F. (1994) *Ben and Jerry's: The Inside Scoop* (New York: Crown).

Liemert, K. (1997) Interview with K. Liemert, Umweltschutzbeauftragter, ADtranz (ABB Daimler-Benz Transportation), 26 March 1997.

Leopold, A. (1949) *A Sand County Almanac* (New York: Oxford University Press, 1981).

Lynch, W. (1994) 'Entrepreneurship: The Key to Global Development and Prosperity' (Distinguished Lecture at Pace University Institute of Global Business Strategy, New York, 5 April 1994).

Mannheim, K. (1936) *Ideology and Utopia: An Introduction to the Sociology of Knowledge* (New York: Harcourt Brace and World).

Manstetten, R. (1995) 'Die Einheit und Unvereinbarkeit von Ökologie und Ökonomie', *GAIA: Ecological Perspectives in Science, Humanities, and Economics* 4.1: 40-51.

Marris, P. (1974) *Loss and Change* (New York: Pantheon).

McClelland, D. (1964) *The Roots of Consciousness* (New York: Van Nostrand).

McClelland, D. (1967) *The Activating Society* (New York: The Free Press).

McKinsey & Co. (1991) *The Corporate Response to the Environmental Challenge* (Amsterdam: McKinsey & Co.).

Mueller, I. (1995) 'Environmental Costs: Impact on the German Economy' (Unpublished MBA Research Project Paper; New York: Pace University).

Müller, B. (1997) Interview with A. Müller, Leiter Qualitätsmanagement/ Umweltmanagement, Rudolf Wild Werke, 26 March 1997.

Naess, A. (1986) 'The Deep Ecological Movement: Some Philosophical Aspects', *Philosophical Inquiry* 8.

Neckermann, K. (1997) Interview with K. Neckermann, Umweltschutzbeauftragter, Heidelberg Schloßquell Brauerei, 30 April 1997.

Nietzsche, F. (1968) 'On the Genealogy of Morals', in W. Kaufmann and R.J. Hollingdale (trans.), *Basic Writings of Nietzsche* (New York: Random House).

Nozick, R. (1974) *Anarchy, State and Utopia* (New York: Basic Books).

Oates, W.E., K. Palmer and P.R. Protney (1995) 'Tightening Environmental Standards: The Benefit–Cost or the No-Cost Paradigm?', *Journal of Economic Perspectives* 9.4: 119-32.

OECD (1992) *The Environment Industry: Situation, Prospects, and Government Policies* (Paris: OECD).

Olson, M. (1965) *The Logic of Collective Action* (Cambridge, MA: Harvard University Press).

Pastakia, A. (1996) 'Grassroots Ecopreneurs: Change Agents for a Sustainable Society' (Paper presented at the 5th International Conference of the Greening of Industry Network, Heidelberg, 25–27 November 1996).

Paterson, M. (1996) *Global Warming and Global Politics* (London: Routledge).

Porter, M. (1991) 'America's Green Strategy', *Scientific American* 264: 168.

Porter, M., and C. van der Linde (1995) 'Toward a New Conception of the Environment–Competitiveness Relation', *Journal of Economic Perspectives* 9.4 (Fall 1995): 97-118.

Putnam, R. (1993) 'The Prosperous Community: Social Capital and Economic Growth', *The American Prospect*, Spring 1993: 35-42.

Putnam, R. (1995) 'Our Separate Ways', *People*, 25 September 1995: 123-28.

Ritzenfeld, T. (1997) Interview with T. Ritzenfeld, Umweltschutzbeauftragter, GETRAG, 3 April 1997.

Rob, P. (1996) *Recycling Data-Techniques and Trends* (Cologne: Duales System Deutschland).

Roddick, A. (1991) *Body and Soul* (New York: Crown).

Saghoff, M. (1994) 'Free-Market versus Libertarian Environmentalism', *Critical Review* 6.2-3: 211-30.

Santayana, G. (1957) *Interpretations of Poetry and Religion* (New York: Harper & Row).

Schellmann, E. (1995) 'Environmental Regulations: A Comparison between the US and Germany' (Unpublished MBA Research Project Paper; New York: Pace University).

Schumacher, E. (1973) *Small is Beautiful* (London: Blond & Briggs).

Schumpeter, J.A. (1950) *Capitalism, Socialism, and Democracy* (New York: Harper & Row).

Seifermann, F. (1997) Interview with F. Seifermann, Geschäftsführer, APU GmbH, 24 March 1997.

Serres, M. (1990) *Le contrat naturel* (Paris: Flammarion).

Sessions, G. (1987) 'The Deep Ecology Movement: A Review', *Environmental Review* 9.

Shenk, D. (1997) *Data Smog: Surviving the Information Glut* (New York: Harper–Collins).

Singer, P. (1975) *Animal Liberation* (New York: New York Review/Random House, 2nd edn, 1990).

Singer, P. (1991) 'The Significance of Animal Suffering', in R.M. Baird and S.E. Rosenbaum (eds.), *Animal Experimentation: The Moral Issues* (New York: Prometheus).

Steger, U., and M. Winter (1996), 'Early Warning of Environmentally-Driven Market Changes: A Theoretical Approach and an Empirical Investigation', *Greener Management International* 15 (July 1996): 31-52.

Stevenson, H., M. Roberts and J. Grousbeck (1989) *New Business Ventures and the Entrepreneur* (Homewood, IL: Irwin).

Stone, C. (1974) Should Trees Have Standing? (Los Altos, CA: William Kaupmann).

Sutton, P. (1997) 'Tapping the Sustainability Market', *Greener Management International* 18 (Summer 1997).

Tatsuno, S. (1990) *Created in Japan* (New York: Harper & Row).

Templet, P.H. (1995) 'The Positive Relationship between Jobs, Environment and the Economy', *Spectrum* 68.2 (Spring 1995): 37-45.

Thoreau, H.D. (1854) *Walden or Life in the Woods* (The Variorum Walden; New York: Washington Square Press, 1963).

United Nations Department for Policy Coordination and Sustainable Development Division for Sustainable Development (1997) *Finance for Sustainable Development: The Road Ahead* (New York: United Nations).

Walley, N., and B. Whitehead (1994a) 'It's Not Easy Being Green', *Harvard Business Review*, May/June 1994.

Walley, N., and B. Whitehead (1994b) 'The Challenge of Going Green', *Harvard Business Review*, July/August 1994: 37-50

Walzer, M. (1994) *Thick and Thin: Moral Argument at Home and Abroad* (Notre Dame, IN: University of Notre Dame Press).

Warner, A., and J. Sachs (1995) 'Economic Reform and Global Integration', (Brookings Papers on Economic Activity; Washington, DC: Brookings Institute).

Weizsäcker, E.U. von, A Lovins and L.H. Lovins (1997) *Factor Four: Doubling Wealth, Halving Resource Use* (Report to the Club of Rome; London: Earthscan).

Welk, H. (1997) Interview with H. Welk, Local Environment Control Officer (LECO), ABB Kraftwerksleittechnik GmbH, 18 March 1997.

Wertsch, J.V. (1985) *Culture Communication and Cognition: Vygotskian Perspectives* (Cambridge: Cambridge University Press).

Wittgenstein, L. (1922) *Tractatus Logico-Philosophicus* (London: Routledge & Kegan Paul, 1988).

Index